How To Measure Program Implementation

D1358949

Lynn Lyons Morris
Carol Taylor Fitz-Gibbon

Center for the Study of Evaluation
University of California, Los Angeles

SAGE PUBLICATIONS   Beverly Hills/London

The *Program Evaluation Kit* was developed at the Center for the Study of Evaluation, University of California, Los Angeles. Copyright of this edition is claimed until December 31, 1988. Thereafter all portions of this work covered by this copyright will be in the public domain.

The *Program Evaluation Kit* was developed under a contract with the National Institute of Education, Department of Health, Education and Welfare. However, the opinions expressed herein do not necessarily reflect the position or policy of that agency, and no official endorsement should be inferred.

The *Program Evaluation Kit* is published and distributed by Sage Publications, Inc., Beverly Hills, California under an exclusive agreement with The Regents of the University of California.

For information address:

Sage Publications, Inc.
275 South Beverly Drive
Beverly Hills, California 90212

Sage Publications Ltd
28 Banner Street
London EC1Y 8QE

Printed in the United States of America

International Standard Book Number 0-8039-1066-5
Library of Congress Catalog Card No. 78-58655

THIRD PRINTING

Table of Contents

Acknowledgements

How To Measure Program Implementation is part of the *Program Evaluation Kit,* developed over a three year period as a project of the Center for the Study of Evaluation (CSE), University of California, Los Angeles. The kit contains eight books, each covering a topic commonly confronting evaluators of educational programs. Many people besides the kit's authors contributed either conceptually or through technical support to its eventual publication.

We owe the idea of writing this kit to Marvin C. Alkin, Director of CSE from 1968 to 1975. Eva L. Baker, current Center Director, provided the continuing solid support and lively interest necessary for its completion. Adrianne Bank, first as co-director of the kit project in its early stages and then in her role as the Center's Associate Director, gave us the moral support necessary to traverse the arduous final stages of kit production.

Several staff members aided in the kit's extensive field test—151 sites throughout the United States and Canada. We thank Margeret Dotseth, Richards Smith Williams, and Esther Goldstein for their painstaking work in gathering and organizing field test data. The tone and content of the kit were strongly influenced by the comments of field test participants whose cooperation we gratefully acknowledge.

Significant editorial and conceptual work was done on this particular book by James Burry and Marlene Henerson. Proofreading and indexing were handled by Michael Bastone, assisted by Mark Young.

Kit booklets were extensively reviewed by experts in the areas of evaluation research, methodology, and measurement. Comments about parts of this book were made by Gaea Leinhardt, University of Pittsburgh; Jason Millman, Cornell University; and Robert Stake, University of Illinois. These reviewers not only made valuable suggestions for revision of early drafts, but by either using the materials in classes with students or by discussing translation of technical issues into lay language, they gave the authors a strong sense of the kit's usefulness as both a procedural guide and educational tool.

We wish to thank members of the Center's technical support staff who worked hard to keep manageable the production of such a large work. Donna Anderson Cuvelier carried the major responsibility for typing, organizing, and supervising manuscript preparation. Ruth Paysen ably shouldered part of the burden of typing the extensive manuscript.

Gracious thanks are also due Lou Orsan who provided advice about graphic design in the preparation of the field test draft of the kit and who designed the books finally published.

We wish finally to thank Cheryl Tyler of the UCLA Office of Contracts and Grants who ably ushered the kit through final legal channels toward publication.

Lynn Lyons Morris

Carol Taylor Fitz-Gibbon

Los Angeles, California
August 1978

Chapter 1
An Orientation To Measuring Program Implementation

How To Measure Program Implementation is one component of the *Program Evaluation Kit,* a set of eight "How To" guides intended for use primarily by people who have been assigned the role of *program evaluator.* The program evaluator has the job of scrutinizing and describing an educational or administrative program so that people may work out ways to improve it and/or judge its quality as is. Program evaluation almost always demands *gathering and digesting information* about program status and *sharing it* with the program's planners, staff, or funders.

This book deals with the task of describing a program's *implementation*—how the program looks in operation.[1] *Keeping track of how the program looks in actual practice is one of the program evaluator's major responsibilities.* You cannot evaluate something without describing what that something is.

If you have taken on an evaluation job, therefore, you will need to produce a description of the program that is as rich in detail as possible. Probably this description will need to be written; but even if it is delivered informally, it should highlight the program's *most important features.* This

---

1. In general, *describing program implementation* should be considered synonymous with *measuring attainment of process objectives* or *determining achievement of means-goals,* phrases used by other authors. The book prefers, however, *not* to discuss implementation solely in connection with process *goals* and *objectives.* This is because the primary reason for measuring implementation in many evaluations is to describe the program that is occurring—whether or not this matches what was planned. Other times, of course, measurement will be directed solely by pre-specified process goals. *Describing program implementation* is a broad enough term to cover both situations.

means it should include a description of the *context* in which the program was initiated—its participants and setting—as well as its unique component *materials* and *activities*.

Circumstances might also demand that you collect *backup data* to support the accuracy of your description.

This book has three purposes:

1. To list for you the program features and activities you might attend to and describe in a program implementation report
2. To help you decide *how much effort* to spend on describing program implementation
3. To guide you in designing instruments to produce backup data so that you can assure yourself and your audience that the description is accurate

This chapter discusses the reasons for examining a program's implementation. Chapter 2 provides an outline for the implementation section of an evaluation report. Using this outline as a guide, you can produce a detailed description of the program based on your answers to the probes accompanying each heading. Chapters 3 through 7 comprise the "How To Measure" section of the book. Chapters 3, 4, 5, and 6 describe methods of measurement—examination of records, observations, interviews, questionnaires—and Chapter 7 discusses validity and reliability, factors reflecting the quality of the measures.

The overall objective of this book is to help you develop skills in describing program implementation and in designing and using appropriate measurement instruments to back up your description. The guidelines in the book are based on the experience of evaluators at the Center for the Study of Evaluation, University of California, Los Angeles, on advice from experts in the fields of educational measurement and evaluation, and on comments of people in school, district, and state settings who used a field test edition of the book.

Whenever possible, procedures in the "How To" sections are presented step-by-step to give you maximum practical advice with minimum theoretical clutter. Many of the recommended procedures, however, are methods for measuring program implementation under *idealized circumstances*. Few evaluation situations, of course, match the ideal. *You should not expect to be able, therefore, to duplicate exactly the suggestions in this book.* It is hoped that you will examine the principles and examples provided, and adapt them to the press of *your* constraints and *your* data requirements. Since many evaluation situations are less than ideal for gathering absolutely unassailable information about programs or program components, the goal of the evaluator should be to provide the best information *possible*. This means gathering the most credible information allowable in your circumstances and presenting your conclusions so as to make them most useful to each of your evaluation audiences.[2]

Why Look At Program Implementation?

In the course of an evaluation, an evaluator might spend a great deal of time and energy measuring and discussing the *attitudes* of parents, administrators, teachers and students, and the *achievement* brought about by a particular program. These are all activities that focus on the impact of an educational endeavor on people or groups. This focus reflects a decision to judge program effectiveness by looking at *outcomes*, asking such questions as: *What results did that program produce? How well are these students doing now? Do parents seem to like what is going on in the district?*

Most people who read an evaluation report assume that the outcomes described by the evaluator *have been brought about* by some orchestrated *set of materials and activities* that has directed the behavior of students, or teachers, or administrators. In the case of students, for example, readers assume that the books they were required to read, the lectures they were required to attend, the practice they were required to engage in, and the field trips they were required to take have summed their various influences to eventually produce the end-of-year achievement scores. These *processes* form the *program* whose outcomes are under scrutiny. The title of a particular program, in fact, often gives not only an idea of the program's intended outcomes, but also a first clue about the activities, materials, or administrative arrangements it encompasses. *Accelerated Math,* for example, evokes images of advanced texts, precocious students, and specially trained teachers. Program titles such as *Mainstreaming of the Educationally Handicapped, Management-by-Objectives,* or *Project Catch-Up-Get-Ahead,* similarly, evoke images of major program components.

The essential purpose behind doing an evaluation, usually, is to answer the question "Does the unique amalgam of materials, activities, administrative arrangements and role-determined tasks that comprise this particular program seem to lead to its achieving its objectives?" Suppose your own

---

2. *Audience* is an important concept in evaluation. The audience is the evaluator's boss; she is its information gatherer. Unless she is writing a report that will not be read, every evaluator has at least one audience. Many evaluations have several. *An audience is a person or group who needs the information from the evaluation for a distinct purpose.* Administrators who want to keep track of program installation because they need to monitor the political climate constitute one potential audience. Curriculum developers who want data about how much achievement a particular program component is producing comprise another. Every audience needs different information; and, importantly, *each maintains different criteria for what it will accept as believable, credible information.*

evaluation data support a resounding *yes* to that question. "It worked!" you might say. Unless you have taken care, however, to describe the program's myriad facets, you will be unable to answer the question that logically follows your judgment of program success. That question would ask: "*What* worked?" If you cannot answer that question, you will have wasted effort measuring the outcomes of an event which cannot be described and must therefore remain a mystery.

But you will be in good company; few evaluation reports pay enough attention to describing the program *processes* which helped participants achieve certain outcomes. For example, some evaluation reports assume that mentioning the title of the project and the source of funds will provide a sufficient description. Other reports devote pages and pages to tables of *Types of Students Participating* or *Teachers Receiving In-Service Training by Subject Matter Area* on the assumption that these data will adequately describe the program's processes for the reader. Though some reports do provide a short description of the program's major features— such as materials developed or purchased, teacher and student in-class activities, employment of aides, administrative supports, and provisions for special training—after reading such a report the reader is often left with only a vague notion of how often or for what duration particular activities occurred, or how ingredients combined to affect daily life in the class-room, school, or district.

A detailed implementation report, intended for people unfamiliar with the program, should include some attention to program characteristics such as those listed in Table 1.

To compound the problem of insufficient description of processes, evaluation reports seldom tell *where and how information about program implementation was obtained*. If the information came from the most usual sources—the project proposal or a conversation with the project director—then some attempt should have been made to determine whether the program that was described in the proposal or during conversations *matched the program that actually occurred*. Few evaluations give a clear picture of what the program that took place actually looked like and, among those few evaluations that do provide a picture of the program, most do not give enough attention to verifying that the picture is an accurate one.

Reports about the implementation of a program should, where possible, include backup data to support program description. Such data would address topics like those listed in Table 1.

It could be argued that this lack of attention to detail and accuracy is justifiable in situations where no one is likely to want to know about the exact features of the program. This is a bogus argument. The fact is that *you cannot interpret a program's results without knowing about its implementation*. For one thing, an evaluation that ignores implementation will

TABLE 1
Topics Covered by a Thorough Implementation Report

Descriptions of Program Characteristics

Background and contextual information about the program. For example, the place of origin of the program; the nature of the program sites—their demographic characteristics and political atmosphere; the breadth of participation per site; how need for the program was determined; the relationship between the program chosen or designed and the goals and objectives of its constituency; the historical background of the program; its target student group; the background, qualifications, and activities of program personnel; administrative features.

Critical features of the program. For example, the budget for program implementation; what materials are used and how they have been selected or developed; the physical setting of instruction; student activities; grouping of students for instructional purposes; teacher-pupil ratio; teacher preparation for program; schedule of program activities; the level of parent and community involvement; overall program rationale.

Backup Data To Support Descriptions

Implementation measures. For example, representativeness of program features discussed; reason for selection of a program feature for examination; methods and bases of instrument development or selection; qualifications of instrument administrators; quality and limitations of the measures used; data collection procedures.

Discussion of program implementation. For example, amount of program life covered by the report; if there is a comparison group, the kinds and degree of differences and similarities between the two groups and the programs they are receiving; kinds of decisions made, by whom; degree of program variation; the "typical" program experience; future program development and/or evaluation.

---

throw together results from sites where the program has been conscientiously installed with those from places which might have decided "Let's not, and say we did." If achievement or attitude results from the overall evaluation are discouraging, then what's to be done? This scenario typifies a poor evaluation study. Unfortunately, it describes many large-scale national program evaluations during the last decade, including a few of those most notorious for showing "no effect" from expensive Federal programs, such as the 1970 evaluation of Project Follow-Through.[3] What is more, ignoring implementation—even when a thorough program description is not explicitly required—means that information has been lost.

---

3. This issue is discussed at greater length, with particular attention to the Follow-Through evaluation in Patton, M. Q. *Utilization-focused evaluation.* Beverly Hills: Sage Publications, 1978 (pp. 149-177).

This information, if properly collected, interpreted, and presented, could have provided audiences (who are becoming increasingly attentive to and demanding of evaluations) with a picture of what good and poor education look like.

It should be clear by now that:

- Description, in as much detail as possible, of the materials, activities, and administrative arrangements that characterized a particular program, is an essential part of its evaluation.
- An adequate description of a program includes backup data from different sources to ensure thoroughness and accuracy.

How much attention *you* choose to give to implementation in your own unique situation, then, substantially affects the quality of your evaluation.

What and How Much To Describe?

A quick look at Chapter 2 should show you that assembling information and writing a detailed implementation report about even a small program could be an impossible job for one person who must work within time constraints. To help you in such a situation, the remainder of the chapter poses some questions to focus your thinking about what to look at, measure, and report. Considering these questions *before* you make decisions about measuring implementation should help ensure that you spend the right amount of time and effort describing the program, and use the measures most appropriate to your circumstances.

Before planning data collection about program implementation, you will need to make two decisions:

1. *Which features of the program is it most critical or valuable for me to describe?* This can amount to deciding *which* sections of the outline in Chapter 2 to use. Your answer will depend, in part, on how much time and money you have. It will also be affected by your role vis-à-vis the staff and the funding agency, the announced major components of the program, and the amount of variation allowed by its planners.
2. *How much and what kind of backup data will be necessary to support the accuracy of the description of each program component?* Decisions about backup evidence will determine whether your report simply announces the existence of a program feature or offers evidence to support the description you have written. This decision will also be constrained by time and money as well as by your own judgments about the need for corroboration and the amount of variation you have found in the program.

If you feel that your experience with evaluation or with the program, its staff, or the funding agency is sufficient to allow you to make these decisions right now, then proceed to Chapter 2 and beyond and begin your data collection.

The three questions that follow are intended to give you further guidance toward decisions concerning what to look at and how to back up your report. These questions relate to: (1) deciding whether you need to document or *monitor* the program, and why; (2) determining the most critical features of the program you are evaluating; and (3) finding out how much variation there is in the program.

Question 1. What Purposes Will Your Implementation Study Serve?

This question asks you to consider your *role* with regard to the program. Your role is primarily determined by the *use* to which the implementation information you supply will be put. The question of use will override any other you might ask about program implementation.

If you have responsibility for producing a *summary statement* about the general effectiveness of the program, then you will probably report to a funding agency, a government office, or some other representative of the program's constituency. You may be expected to describe the program, to produce a statement concerning the program's achievement of its intended goals, to note unanticipated outcomes, and possibly to make comparisons with an alternative program. If these tasks resemble the features of your job, you have been asked to assume the role of *summative* evaluator.

On the other hand, your evaluation task may characterize you as a *helper* and *advisor* to the program planners and developers. During the early stages of the program in operation, you may be called on to describe and monitor program activities, periodically test for progress in achievement or attitude change, look out for potential problems, and identify areas where the program needs improvement. You may or may not be required to produce a formal report at the end of your activities. In this situation, you are a "trouble-shooter" and a problem solver, a person whose overall task is not well-defined. If these more loosely-defined tasks resemble the features of your job, you are a *formative evaluator*.

Sometimes an evaluator is asked to assume both roles at once—a difficult, hectic, but still possible assignment.

While concerns of both the formative and summative evaluator focus on collecting information and reporting to appropriate groups, the measurement and description of program implementation within each evaluation role varies greatly, so greatly that different names are used to characterize the two kinds of implementation focus. Description of program implementation for *summative* evaluation is usually called *program documentation*. A documentation of a program is its official description outlining the fixed critical features of the program as well as diverse variations that might have been allowed. *Documentation* connotes something well-defined and solid. Documentation of a program, and its summative evaluation, should occur only after the program has had sufficient time to correct problems and function smoothly.

On the other hand, description of program implementation for formative evaluation will be termed *program monitoring* in this book. Monitoring connotes something more active and less fixed than documentation. The more fluid connotation of monitoring reflects the evolving nature of the program and its formative evaluation requirements. The formative evaluator's job is not only to describe the program, but also *to keep a vigilant watch over its development* and *to call the attention of the program staff to what is happening.* Program monitoring in formative evaluation should reveal to what extent the program as implemented matches what its planners intended, and should provide a basis for deciding whether parts of the program ought to be improved, replaced, or augmented. Formative evaluation occurs while the program is still developing and can be modified on the basis of evaluation findings.

Measuring implementation for program documentation

Part of the task of the summative evaluator is to record, for external distribution, an official description of what the program looked like in operation. This program documentation might be used for the following purposes:

1. *Accountability*. Sometimes the expected outcomes of a program, such as heightened independence among learners, are intangible and difficult to measure. At other times program outcomes may be remote and

occur at some time in the future after the program has concluded and its participants have moved on. This kind of outcome, concerned, for instance, with such matters as responsible citizenship or career success is not expected to reach consummate achievement by the participants during the program. Rather, the program is intended to move its participants *toward* achievement of the objective. In such instances, where judging the program completely on the basis of outcomes might be impractical or even unfair, program evaluation can focus primarily on *implementation*. Program staff can be held accountable for at least providing materials and producing activities that should help people progress toward future goals. Alternative school programs, treatment programs for disturbed or exceptional students, programs responding to desegregation mandates, and other programs involving shifts of personnel or students are some examples of cases where evaluation might well focus principally on implementation. Though these programs might result in remote or fuzzy learning outcomes, the nature of their proper implementation can often be precisely specified.

Of course, implementation might need to be measured to support accountability in any case. Even when a program's objectives *are* immediate and can be readily measured, it is likely that the staff will be accountable for some amount of implementation of intended program features. They will need to show, in other words, where the money has gone.

2. *Providing a lasting description of the program.* The summative evaluator's written report may be the only description of the program remaining after it has terminated. This report should therefore provide

an accurate account of the program and include sufficient detail so that it can serve as a basis for planning by those who may want to reinstate the program in some revised form or at another site. Such future audiences of your report need to know the characteristics of the site and the sorts of materials and activities that probably brought about the program's outcomes.

3. *Providing a list of the possible causes of the program's effects.* A summative evaluation which uses a highly credible design and valid measures of outcomes constitutes a research study. It can serve as a test of the hypothesis that the particular set of activities and materials incorporated in the program produces good achievement and attitudes. Here the summative report about a particular program has something to say to policy makers about programs using similar processes or aiming toward the same goals. The activities and materials described in the evaluator's documentation, in this case, are the independent, or manipulated, variables in an educational experiment.

Knowing the uses to which your documentation will be put helps you to determine how much effort to invest in it. Implementation information collected for the purpose of *accountability* should focus on those activities, administrative changes, or materials *that are either specifically required by the program funders or have been put forward by the program's planners as major vehicles for producing its beneficial effects.*

The *amount of detail* with which you describe these characteristics will depend, in turn, on how precisely planners or funders have specified what should take place. If planners, for instance, have prescribed only that a program should use the XYZ Reading Series, measuring implementation will require examining the extent of use of this series. If, on the other hand, it is planned that certain *portions* of the series be used with children having, say, problems with reading comprehension, then describing implementation will require that you look at *which* portions are being used, and *with whom*. You will probably need to look at test scores to ensure that the proper students are using XYZ. The program might *further* specify that teachers working in XYZ with problem readers carry out a daily 10-minute drill, rhythmically reading aloud, in a group, a paragraph from the XYZ story for the week. If the program has been planned *this specifically*, then your program description will probably need to attend to these details as well. As a matter of fact, attention to specific behaviors is a good idea when describing any program *where you see certain behavior occurring routinely.* Program descriptions at the level of teacher and student behavior help readers to visualize what students have experienced, giving them a good chance to think about what it is that has helped the students to learn.

If accountability is the major reason for your summative evaluation, then you must provide *backup data* to show whether—and to what extent—the program's most important events actually did occur. The more skeptical your audience, the greater the necessity for providing formal backup data. Concerns about the skeptical audience are elaborated in later questions in this chapter.

If you need to provide a *permanent record* of program implementation for the purpose of its eventual replication or expansion, try to cover as many as possible of the program characteristics listed in Chapter 2. The level of detail with which you describe each program feature should equal or exceed the specificity of the program plan, *at least when describing the features that the staff considers most crucial to producing program effects.* If additional practices typical of the program should come to your attention while conducting your evaluation, you should include these. You will need to use sufficient backup data so that neither you nor your audience doubt the accuracy or generality of your description.

When describing implementation for the purposes of accountability and leaving a lasting record of a program, the backup data you collect *can* be fairly *informal*, depending on your audience's willingness to believe you. You might talk with staff members, peruse school records, drop in on class sessions, or quote from the program proposal.

In cases where the reason for measuring implementation involves *research*, or where there is potential for *controversy* about your data and conclusions, you will need to back up your description of the program through *systematic measurement*, such as coded observations by trained raters, examination of program records, structured interviews, or questionnaires. Carefully planned and executed measurement will allow you to be reasonably certain that the information you report truly describes the situation at hand. It is important that the evaluator produce formal measures in cases where he himself wants to verify the accuracy of his program description. It is essential that he measure if he thinks he will need to *defend* his description of the program, that is, if he might confront a skeptic. An example from a common situation should illustrate this.

Example. Charles Wong, working for the Evaluation Office of the State Department of Education, was assigned to evaluate statewide facilities in special education for trainable mentally retarded (TMR) students. Dr. Wong sent a lengthy questionnaire early in the school year to 235 sites, requesting the chief administrator to describe physical facilities, staff qualifications, student characteristics, and the educational/vocational/recreational programs carried out. Based on the questionnaire, Dr. Wong prepared a summary report, parts of which were reported in newspapers statewide.

The State Association for Retarded Children, however, took issue with the study's findings. Programs, it claimed, did not by and large operate according to the clear objectives described in the report, nor were facilities as well equipped as the report implied. In response to these serious charges, the State Department directed Dr. Wong to follow up his questionnaire with interviews and observations from a random sample of TMR sites.

What he found—mainly on the basis of observations made by trained raters using checklists he had developed—was that facilities were indeed as well equipped as their administrators had originally said and that the curriculum was organized around worthwhile goals. Day-to-day *classroom practice,* however, made poor use of available equipment and was only roughly keyed to the highly specific and well stated objectives which most of the sites had copied from the state's own TMR program guidelines. Mr. Wong could only discover what was actually going on by taking eyes and ears to the program sites themselves.

Measuring implementation for program monitoring

As has been mentioned, the task of the formative evaluator is more varied than that of the summative evaluator. Formative evaluation involves not only the critical activities of examining and reporting about student progress and monitoring implementation, it also often means assuming a role in the program's planning, development, and refinement. The formative evaluator's responsibilities specifically related to program implementation usually include the following:

1. *Ensuring, throughout program development, that the program's official description is kept up-to-date, reflecting how the program is actually being conducted.* While for small-scale programs, this description could be unwritten and agreed upon by the few active staff members, most programs should be described in a written outline which is periodically updated. An outline of program processes written before implementation is usually called a *program plan.* Recording what has taken place during the program's implementation produces one or more *formative implementation reports.* The task of providing formative implementation reports—and often ensuring the existence of a coherent program plan as well—falls to the formative evaluator.

   The topics discussed in the formative report could coincide with the headings in the implementation report outline in Chapter 2. *The amount of detail in which each aspect of the program is described should match the level of detail of the program plan.*

   In many situations, the formative evaluator finds his first task to be clarification of the program plan. After all, if he is to help the staff improve the program as it develops, he and they need to have a clear idea at the outset of how it is supposed to look. If you plan to work as a formative evaluator, do not be surprised to find that the staff has only a vague planning document. Unless the program relies heavily on commercially published materials with accompanying procedural guides, or the program planners are experienced curriculum developers, planners have probably taken a wait-and-see attitude about many of the program's critical features. This attitude need not be bothersome; as long as it does not mask hidden disagreements among staff members about how to proceed, or cover up uncertainty about the program's objectives, a tentive attitude toward the program can be healthy. It allows the program to take on the form that will work best. It gives you, however, the job of *recording* what *does* happen so that when and if summative evaluation takes place, it will focus on a realistic depiction of the program. An accurate portrayal of the program will also be useful to those who plan to adopt, adapt, or expand the program in the future.

2. *Helping the staff and planners to change and add to the program as it develops.* In many instances the formative evaluator will become involved in program planning—or at least in designing changes in the program as it assumes cleaner form. How involved she becomes will depend on the situation. If a program has been planned in considerable detail, and if planners are experienced and well versed in the program's subject matter, then they may want the formative evaluator only to provide information about whether the program is deviating from the program plan.

On the other hand, if planners are inexperienced, or if the program was not planned in great detail in the first place, then the evaluator becomes an investigative reporter. Her first job might be to find out what is happening—to see what is going well and badly in the program. She will need to examine the program's activities independent of guidance from the plan, and then help eliminate weaknesses and expand on the program's good points. If this case fits your situation, use the list of implementation characteristics in Chapter 2 as a set of suggestions about what to look for, or adopt a responsive/naturalistic approach described later.

The formative evaluator's service to a staff that wants to change and improve its program could result in diverse activities. Two of them are particularly important:

a. The formative evaluator could provide information that prompts the staff and planners to reflect periodically on whether the program that is evolving is the one they want to have. This is necessary because programs installed at a particular site practically never look as they did on paper—or as they did when in operation elsewhere. At the same time, staff and planners will be persuaded to re-examine their initial thinking about *why* the processes they have chosen to implement will lead to attaining their objectives. Careful examination of a program's *rationale*, handled with sensitivity to the program's setting, could turn out to be the greatest service of a formative evaluator. The planners should have in mind a sensible notion of cause and effect relating the desired outcomes to the program-as-envisioned. Insofar as the program-as-implemented and the outcomes observed fail to match expectations, the program's rationale may have to be revised.

b. Controversies over alternative ways to implement the program might lead the formative evaluator to conduct small-scale *pilot studies,* attitude surveys, or experiments with newly-developed program materials and activities. Program planners, after all, must constantly make decisions about how the program will look. These decisions are usually based only on hunches about what will work best or will be accepted most readily. For instance: *Should all math instruction take place in one session, or should there be two sessions during the day? How much discussion in the vocational education course should precede field trips? How much should follow? Will practice on the Controlled Reading Machine produce results that are as good as those obtained when children tutor one another? How much additional paperwork will busy teachers tolerate? How much worksheet activity can be included in the French course without detracting from students' chances of attaining high conversational fluency?*
    These are good and reasonable questions which can be answered by means of quick opinion surveys or short experiments, using the methods described in most texts on the topic of research design.[4]

---

4. See, for instance, Fitz-Gibbon, C. T., & Morris, L. L. How to design a program evaluation. In Morris, L. L. (Ed.), *Program evaluation kit.* Beverly Hills: Sage Publications, 1978. See, as well, the "Step-by-step guide for conducting a small experiment" in Morris, L. L., & Fitz-Gibbon, C. T., Evaluator's handbook, also part of the *Program evaluation kit.*

A short experiment will require that you select experimental and control groups, and then choose treatments to be given to these groups that represent the decision alternatives in question. These short studies should last long enough to allow the alternatives to show effects. The advantage of performing short experiments will quickly become apparent to you; they provide credible evidence about the effectiveness of alternative program components or practices.

Whether you work as a summative or a formative evaluator, you will need to decide how much of your implementation report can rely on anecdotal or conversational information and still be credible, and how much your report needs to be backed up by data produced by formal or systematic *measurement* of program implementation. If what you describe can make a difference to those who might use it for any of the purposes mentioned, then your implementation report deserves all the time and effort you can afford.

Question 2. What Are the Program's Most Critical Characteristics?

Having determined the ways that the information you provide can be used by different audiences with different decision purposes, your identification of the program's *critical features* will help you further to determine:

- *Which* of the more specific questions in Chapter 2's implementation report outline you should address
- *What level of detail* to use in describing the program

You can begin describing the program by outlining the elements of the program's *context*—the tangible features of the program and its setting:

- The classrooms, schools, or districts where the program has been installed
- The program staff—including administrators, teachers, aides, parent volunteers, and secretaries
- The resources used—including materials constructed or purchased, and equipment, particularly that purchased especially for the program
- The students—including the particular characteristics that made them eligible for the program, their number, and their level of competency at the beginning of the program

These context features constitute the *bare bones* of the program and must be included in any summary report. Listing them usually does not require much data gathering on your part, since they are not the sort of data that you expect anyone to challenge or view with skepticism. Unless you have doubts about the delivery of materials, or you think that the wrong staff members or students may be participating, there is little need for backup data to support your description.

In addition to describing context features, however, you will need to devote some time to examining and reporting the *activities* in which program staff and participants took part. Describing important activities demands formulating and answering questions about *how* the program was implemented:

- Were the materials used? Were they used as intended?
- What procedures were prescribed for the teachers to follow in their teaching and other interactions with students? Were these procedures followed?
- In what activities were the students in the program supposed to participate? Did they?
- What activities were prescribed for other participants—aides, parents, tutors? Did they engage in them?
- What administrative arrangements did the program include? What lines of authority were to be used for making important decisions? What changes occurred in these arrangements or lines of authority?

Listing the salient activities intended to occur in the program will, of course, take you much less time than verifying that they *have* occurred, and in the form intended. Unlike materials, which usually stay put and whose presence can be checked at practically any time, program activities may be inaccessible once they have occurred if they were not consciously observed or recorded. Counting them or merely noting their presence is therefore no small task. In addition, activities are more difficult to *recognize* than context features. Math games, teaching machines, aides, and science materials from Company X are easily identified; but what exactly does the act of *reinforcement* or *acceptance of a student's cultural background* look like when it is taking place?

Occurrence of intangible activities such as reinforcement or cultural acceptance cannot be simply observed and reported like an inventory of materials or a headcount of students. Even if they could be directly observed, you could not possibly describe all of them. *You will have to choose which activities to attend to.* Your choice of these activities will in large measure depend upon what your audience has said it needs to know in order to make informed decisions. In addition to audience needs, three sources of information should help you decide what to examine:

1. The program plan or proposal

2. Opinions of experts, consultants, program personnel, and yourself, based on hunches about what works

3. Your own observations

Picking out critical program features from the plan or proposal

Some program proposals will come right out and list the program's most important features, perhaps even explaining *why* planners think these materials and activities will bring about the desired outcomes. But many will not, although if you look carefully, you may find clues about what is considered important. For instance, most proposals or documents describing a program will refer over and over to certain *key activities* which should occur. As a rule of thumb, the more frequently an activity is cited, the more critical someone considers it to be for program success. You may therefore decide that activities *repeatedly mentioned* are critical program components to which the evaluation must attend.

The program's *budget* is another index to its crucial features. As another rule of thumb, you might assume that the larger the budgeted dollar or other resource expenditure, such as staffing level, for a particular program feature–activity, event, material, or configuration of program elements–the greater its presumed contribution to program success. Taken together, these two planning elements–frequency of citation and level of expenditure or effort–can provide some indication of the program's most critical components.

Relying on the program plan for suggestions about *what* needs to be described determines a point of view from which to approach your implementation evaluation. *An implementation evaluation based largely on the program plan will involve collecting data to determine the extent to which the crucial activities named by the plan occurred as intended*–and if they did not occur as planned, what happened instead. Description of a program from this point of view is the kind most often done, and for an understandable reason: it provides the simplest means by which the evaluator can decide which activities to look at.

Example. A group of health and science teachers wrote a proposal to the state for a few thousand dollars to assemble a personal hygiene and sex education course for Rogus City's high schools. The program was to be based largely on purchased audio-visual materials. The state evaluator who examined the program relied heavily on the original proposal as a program descriptor. To complete the documentation section of his summative report, he simply noted the program's official description, and observed informally to locate consistencies and discrepancies between the planned program and the one that actually occurred.

Even in the absence of a formal written program plan, documentation from the perspective of implicit planning can be done by *interviewing program planners* and asking them to describe activities they feel are crucial to the program. You can then proceed with the documentation of the extent of occurrence of these activities.

You might find the program plan and even the planners themselves, in some instances, to be disappointing sources of ideas about what to look for. They might not describe proposed activities to the degree of specificity you feel you need; or they might express grandiose plans, engendered by initial enthusiasm, or in response to proposal guidelines from the funding source which were themselves overly ambitious. It is possible, as well, that the program *has not been planned* in any specific way.

How then will you document the program if, for whatever reason, there is no plan which details activities that are specific, feasible, and consistent throughout? In this case, you have two options: you can rely on what *theory* and *experienced people* say should be in the program; or you can take the point of view of a *responsive/naturalistic observer*[5] and simply watch the program operating to discover what seems to be the program's critical features.

Relying on opinions and hunches of experts, program personnel, consultants and yourself

If you have reason to believe that some feature *not mentioned* in the program's planning documents might be necessary for program success, then look for it. Commonly unmentioned but critical program characteristics, for instance, are *rehearsal or repetition of learned information,* and *adequate time on task.* Planners of instructional programs, it seems, spend a lot of time deciding what to teach and in what sequence, but often overlook students' need to repeat and study the information they have received.

Whether or not the kinds of characteristics or program activities mentioned above are critical in *your* situation, *you should give consideration to features, not specifically cited in the program plan, whose presence or absence might be related to program success or failure.* If you are a formative evaluator, it is, in fact, your responsibility to bring these matters to the attention of the staff. You might, incidentally, discover a feature of the program that someone thinks could actually make it fail. By all means, pay attention to this kind of information, backing up your description with data.

---

5. This term, and its methodological ramifications, are described on pages 29 to 31.

Example. Mr. Walker, the director and *de facto* formative evaluator of in-service training programs at a university-based Teacher Center, noticed that some districts sending teachers allowed them free choice of courses. Others, believing that in-service training should follow a theme, encouraged teachers to take courses within a single area—say elementary math, or affective education.

Though the Teacher Center itself made no recommendations about what courses should be pursued, Mr. Walker decided that the "theme versus no-theme" flavor of teacher training might have an effect on teachers' overall assessment of the value of their in-service experiences. He decided to describe the course of study of the two groups of teachers at the Center and separately analyze the groups' responses to an attitude questionnaire.

As Mr. Walker expected, teachers whose training followed a theme expressed greater enthusiasm about the Teacher Center. Since he could find no explanation for the difference in enthusiasm between the two groups other than the thematic character of one group's program, Mr. Walker recommended that the Center itself encourage thematic in-service study. He used his descriptions of the courses of study of the teachers in the theme group as a set of models the Center might follow.

To the extent that you base your choice of what to look for on a theory of what works in education, you are conducting what has been called *Theory-Based Evaluation.*[6] Mr. Walker, in the example above, worked from the rather rudimentary but verifiable theory that education that follows a program of study is more likely to be perceived by the student as valuable. His evaluation was at least partly theory-based because he used a theory to tell him what to look at.

Examining program implementation in theory-based evaluation gives your study a point of view toward the program similar to the one you assume when basing implementation measurement on the proposal: you begin with a *prescription* of what effective program activities might look like. The prescription from the theory based perspective, however, comes not from a written plan, but from a theory.

A theory-based implementation evaluation is especially appropriate for looking at a school program that is built on a *model* of teaching behavior; *theory* of learning, development, or human behavior; or *philosophy* concerning children, schools, or organizations. The specific prescriptions of many such models and theories are familiar to most people working in education.[7]

---

6. Fitz-Gibbon, C. T., & Morris, L. L. Theory-based evaluation. *Evaluation Comment,* 1975, *5*(1), 1-4.

7. An excellent presentation of the implications of various models of schooling and education is put forth in Joyce, B., & Weil, M. *Models of teaching.* Englewood Cliffs, NJ: Prentice-Hall, 1972. See, as well, Kohl, H. The open classroom. New York: Random House, 1969 and also Neill, A. S. *Summerhill.* New York: Hart, 1960.

Examples of some of these models are:

- Behavior modification and various applications of reinforcement theory to instruction and classroom discipline
- Piaget's theory of cognitive development and other models of how children learn concepts
- Open-classroom and free-school models such as those put forth by writers in education in the 1960's
- Fundamental-school and basic skills models which seek to reinstate traditional American classroom practices
- Models of organizations that prescribe arrangements and procedures for effective management

A program identified with any of these points of view must set up roles and procedures consistent with the particular theory or value system. Proponents of open schools, for instance, would agree that a classroom reflecting their point of view should display freedom of movement, individualization of instruction, and curricular choices made by students. Each theory, philosophy, or teaching model contends that *particular activities* are either worthwhile in and of themselves or are the best way to promote certain desirable outcomes. Measuring implementation of a theory-based program, then, becomes a matter of checking the extent to which activities or organizational arrangements at the program sites reflect the theory.

Recently, Cooley and Lohnes have proposed a *general model* of school learning[8] that seems particularly useful as a source of ideas for what to look at when describing a program intended to *teach* people something. The effectiveness of school programs in bringing about desired learning, according to this model, depends on four factors:

1. *Learning opportunities.* Schools provide the time and place in which students may practice new skills, attend to sources of new information, or come in contact with models of how to act.

2. *Motivation.* Schools intentionally manipulate rewards and punishments that persuade students to pursue prescribed activities and attend to particular information.

3. *Structured presentation of activities, ideas, and information.* Schools attempt to organize and sequence what is presented, tailoring it to students' abilities so as to make learning as painless and efficient as possible.

4. *Instructional events.* The school day is filled with social and interpersonal contacts that promote learning. The elimination of misunder-

8. Cooley, W. W., & Lohnes, P. R. *Evaluation research in education.* New York: Irvington Publishers, 1976.

standings through dialogue, a teacher's effective use of student contributions in a class discussion, and the personal attention and reassurance that prevent student discouragement are some examples of instructional events in this sense.

Figure 1 shows a simple diagram of the Cooley/Lohnes model. Opportunity, motivators, structure, and instructional events change the student from his level of initial performance to the criterion performance desired for the program. The important thing about the Cooley/Lohnes model for describing program implementation is that each of these four aspects of schooling involves critical features that an evaluator might want to mention when describing a program.

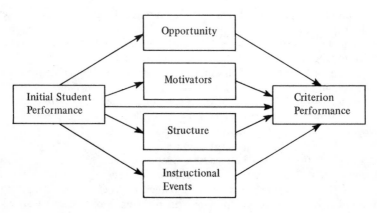

Figure 1. A model of classroom processes[9]

Some evaluators have shown that different philosophies about school and classroom processes can be described and compared nicely using the four dimensions of the Cooley/Lohnes model.[10] In looking at program implementation, an evaluator can ask questions such as the following:

- *Opportunity:* What materials addressing the program objectives were available to students? How much time was allotted to learning and practicing the target skills and understandings? How did conditions affecting opportunity, such as attendance, access to materials, and distractions from relevant learning activi-

---

9. Reprinted from Cooley, W. W., & Lohnes, P. R. *Evaluation research in education.* New York: Irvington Publishers, 1976, p. 191.

10. Leinhardt, G. Applying a classroom process model to instructional evaluation. *Curriculum Inquiry,* 1978, *8*(2).

ties, vary across sites or among students? Did learning opportunities vary *intentionally* in duration and nature? If so, were differences specified by the program, or left to teachers or students to determine?

- *Motivators:* Were the materials capable of maintaining student attention or interest? Was a reinforcement system used? What systems of reward or punishment were used, and were parents involved? Did success with motivation techniques vary across sites? What conditions might have had a bearing on the different levels of motivation among students?

- *Structure:* To what extent were program objectives specified? Were learning hierarchies used to underlie the curriculum? Was a coherent outline used? How much attention was paid to sequencing of lessons? Was there an in-service program to teach novel subject matter, and were teachers aware of the rationale behind program sequencing? What efforts were made to ensure that program objectives and instruction would be suitable in terms of students' backgrounds and abilities?

- *Intructional Events:* What interpersonal contacts were there that tended to support student involvement in program activities? How much personal attention did individual students receive? Was instruction one-to-one or one-to-many? Businesslike or friendly? Frequent or infrequent? Primarily between students and teachers, students and students, or students and aides?

Theory-based evaluation might also involve your assessment of the consistency of the program *plan* with the underlying theory.

In summative evaluations based on a credible research design, you should note, a theory-based evaluation can provide an actual *test* of the theory's validity. Given the potential importance, and rarity, of empirical validation of a theory, results of an evaluation which has provided such validation should be reported and disseminated as widely as possible.

Responsive[11]/naturalistic observations and case studies

It is possible for an evaluator to observe the program in operation with relatively few preconceptions or decisions about what to look for. This strategy might be chosen for a number of reasons. For one thing, some evaluators consider it the best way of describing a program. Unhampered by preconceptions and prescriptions, the responsive/naturalistic inquirer might set his sights on catching the true flavor of a program, discovering the unique set of elements that make it work, and conveying them to the evaluation's audience. Further, a naturalistic approach might be necessary if there is no written plan for the program you are evaluating and you find that one cannot be retrospectively constructed with a reasonable degree of consistency by the planners. Even if there is a plan, it might be vague or,

11. The responsive/naturalistic approach to describing program events has been most fully described and advocated by Robert Stake. Responsive evaluations (a) use naturalistic methods for examining the program to be evaluated, and (b) avoid preconceptions about *what* the evaluator will finally describe.

from your perspective, unrealistic to implement. Then again, you might discover that the program has been allowed so much variation from site to site that common features are not apparent at first. In any of these cases, you have the option of just observing.

Implicit in your decision to use responsive methods are two other decisions:

1. To rely heavily on data collection methods that "get close to the data," usually classroom observations
2. To concentrate on relating what you found, rather than comparing what was to what should have been.

This might leave you up in the air at first about what to look for.

Example. The School Board of a small city decided that high schools should spend one year emphasizing Language Arts, with particular focus on improving students' writing skills. The district's Assistant Superintendent for Curriculum resisted the initial impulse to design and implement a common, districtwide program. Instead, she decided that each teacher should be allowed to respond, in his or her own way, to the basic decision to emphasize writing. Her reasoning was that some teachers would arrive at good methods that the other teachers could use to everyone's advantage—students and teachers alike. To keep track of what teachers were doing, however, she scheduled periodic teacher and student interviews and dropped in on class sessions frequently. She wrote vignettes describing classroom practices she had seen and which reflected the aspirations and reports of teachers and students. Her report demonstrated to the Board the effects of its priority decision; and circulated among teachers in abbreviated form, it served as a source of new teaching ideas.

This scenario might look familiar to you. The evaluator's vignettes correspond to how most people share information; and indeed, a responsive evaluation in a context that is free from controversy or skepticism looks very much like what people usually do. The difference between this evaluation, however, and a formal responsive evaluation is in the quality of the observations made. Responsive evaluators use methods from the social sciences—notably anthropology—to obtain corroboration for their observations and conclusions. They have, in fact, developed a method for conducting evaluations that follows that of naturalistic field studies.

An evaluation using a naturalistic method would follow a scenario something like this:

1. A particular program is to be evaluated. If there are numerous sites, one or more sites is chosen for study.

2. The evaluator observes activities at the site or sites chosen, perhaps even taking part in the activities, but trying to influence the program routine as little as possible. Often, time constraints require the use of "informants"—people who have already been observing things and who can be interviewed.

3. Though data collection could take the form of coded records like those produced through the standard observation methods described in Chapter 5, the responsive/naturalistic observer more often records what he sees in the form of *field notes*. This choice of recording method is motivated mainly by a desire to avoid deciding too soon which aspects of the situation observed will be considered most important.

4. The responsive/naturalistic observer shifts back and forth between formal data collection, study of recorded notes, and informal conversation with the subjects. Gradually she produces a description of the events and direct or indirect interpretation of them. The report is usually an oral or written narrative, though naturalistic studies yield tables, sociograms, and other numerical and graphic summaries as well.

Case studies (considered technically) represent not so much a *method* as a choice of *what* to study. Case study researchers quite often follow naturalistic methodology. The case study worker in evaluation chooses to examine closely a particular case—that is, a school, a classroom, a particular group, or individual experiencing the program. Sometimes the program itself is "the case." Whereas the naturalistic observer or the more traditional evaluator might concentrate only on those experiences of, say, a school, which are related to the program, the case study evaluator will usually be interested in a broader range of events and relationships. If the school is the subject of study, then the job is to describe the school. The case study method places the program within the context of the *many* things which happen to the school, its staff, and its students over the course of the evaluation. One result of this method, you can see, is to display the proportional influence of the program among the myriad other factors influencing the actions and feelings of the people under study. While case studies often use naturalistic methods—presumably because of the complexity of the experiences and encounters which need to be described—it is possible for a case study to use more traditional methods of data collection as well as to subject the case to a contrived situation reminiscent of traditional experiments.

Since responsive evaluation, naturalistic inquiry, and case studies have produced a considerable, and generally non-directive literature, detailed guidelines for conducting naturalistic and case-focused evaluations are not included in this book. While the measurement chapters attempt to mention ways in which certain instruments might be used to further the interest of responsive/naturalistic inquiry or case studies, a full treatment of proper methods for conducting these is not possible here. If you are interested in conducting naturalistic inquiry or a case study, consult the references in the *For Further Reading* section at the end of the chapter.

A listing of the critical features of the program will give you some notion of which questions in Chapter 2 to answer in your implementation report. If you are a summative evaluator, then your task will be to convey to your audience as complete a depiction of the program's crucial characteristics as possible.

If you are a formative evaluator, then your decision about what to look at might have to go a step beyond listing the program's critical features. Since your job is to help with program improvement and not merely to describe the program, your task is to collect information that will be maximally useful *for helping the program staff to improve the program.* In most cases, this will certainly mean monitoring the implementation of the program's most critical features. But you will need to consult with the program staff to find which among all the program's critical features seem most troublesome to them, most in need of vigilant attention, or most amenable to change. It could be, for instance, that a program's most critical feature is employment of aides. But once the aides have arrived and it has been established that they come to work regularly, attention to this detail may not be necessary. Your formative service to the program will be more usefully employed in monitoring the implementation of program aspects about which the staff has genuine problems to solve.

Question 3. How Much Variation Is There in the Program?

Your choice of which program characteristics to describe will be influenced by the *amount of variation* that occurs across sites where the program is being used and variation that happens at different points in time. For one thing, depending on the point of view of the planners, variability might be considered desirable or undesirable. Some programs, after all, *encourage* variation. Directors of such programs have said to the staff or to their delegates at different sites something like the following:

> *The district curriculum office has chosen six reading programs which we can purchase with our new Federal Compensatory Education money. Examine these, and select the one you think best suits your students and teachers.*

It is likely that an evaluator—either formative[12] or summative—will be called in to examine the whole Federal Compensatory Education program,

---

12. Where there is *one* formative evaluator working with the program district-wide, she will become involved with assessing variation and perhaps sharing ideas across sites. Where there is a separate formative evaluator *at each site,* each evaluator will work according to different priorities. The job of each evaluator will be to see that *each* version of the program develops as well as possible, perhaps disregarding what other sites are doing.

and he will probably find six versions of the program taking place. Here variation across sites *has been planned,* and implementation of each reading subprogram will have to be described separately. Where such planned variation occurs, incidentally, the evaluator has a good opportunity to collect information that might be useful for future planning in this district or elsewhere—particularly if the district wants to narrow the number of reading programs to fewer than six. He can compare the ease and accuracy of implementation and success with students of the various programs across sites. Where different programs have been implemented by sites that are otherwise similar, the evaluator can compare results to gain clues about the relative effectiveness of the programs. If programs can be *randomly* distributed to schools, the evaluator will be able to collect even more highly credible, and therefore valuable, information about relative program quality.

Program directors could have allowed the program to vary in an even *less* controlled way by saying:

We have X dollars to improve our reading program for the educationally disadvantaged. Take these funds and put together a new program.

This kind of directive produces a program whose only common features across sites are likely to be the target students and the funding source! While variation is also *planned* in this kind of situation, unlike the program in the preceding example, each site has been left free to create *its own unique program.* The district-wide evaluator will have to look separately at each different version of the program that emerges, probably adopting a theory-based, case study, or responsive/naturalistic method. Though he may find a chance to make comparisons among the program versions put into effect at each site, he will probably spend a great deal of time *discovering* and reporting about what each program variation looked like. However, the simple act of telling the implementors about the various forms the program has taken will be useful. Most probably, some forms of the program will be more easily implemented, produce better results, or be more popular than others.

A program can afford to permit considerable variation across sites only in its early stages when it can make mistakes with minimum fear of penalties. For this reason, dealing with planned variation should be primarily the concern of the formative evaluator whose responsibility would then entail tracking the variations, comparing results of different versions of the program at comparable sites, and sharing information about commendable practices. Unfortunately, funding agencies often request summative reports at a time in the life of a program when considerable variation still exists. When this happens, the summative evaluator should note that several *different* program renditions are being evaluated. He should describe each of these, *and report results separately,* making comparisons where possible.

If the evaluator—whether summative or formative—should uncover variation across sites or over time that has *not* been planned, then he will have to describe this, collecting backup data if he feels that he will need corroborating evidence.

This chapter has discussed the measurement of program implementation with a view toward making this aspect of your evaluation report reflect the needs of your audiences, the context you are working in, and your own professional standards. To help ensure that your reports will be useful and credible, this chapter has been concerned with the critical decisions you should make *before* you begin your evaluation—which features of the program your evaluation should focus on and how you will substantiate your description of the program. To help you with these decisions, your attention has been directed to three key questions:

1. What purposes will your implementation study serve?
2. What are the program's most critical characteristics?
3. How much variation is there in the program?

Your implementation evaluation should be as methodologically sound as you can make it. And, as when dealing with achievement and attitudes, your report should provide *credible* and, above all, *useful* information to your audiences.

For Further Reading

Cooley, W. W., & Lohnes, P. R. *Evaluation research in education.* New York: Irvington Publishers, 1976.

Georgiades, W. *How good is your school?* Reston, VA: The National Association of Secondary School Principals, 1978.

Leinhardt, G. Evaluating an adaptive education program: Implementation to replication. *Instructional Sciences,* 1977, *6,* 223-257.

Patton, M. Q. *Utilization-focused evaluation.* Beverly Hills: Sage Publications, 1978.

Stallings, J. Implementation and child effects of teaching practices in Follow-Through classrooms. *Monographs of the Society for Research in Child Development,* 1975, *40,* 1-119.

On the topic of responsive/naturalistic inquiry and case studies . . .

. . . How to do them

Denzin, N. *The research act.* Chicago: Aldine, 1970.

Schatzman, L., & Strauss, A. *Field research: Strategies for a natural sociology.* Englewood Cliffs, NJ: Prentice Hall, 1973.

Shaw, K. E. Understanding the curriculum: The approach through case studies. *Curriculum Studies,* 1978, *10*(1), 1-17.

Smith, L. M. An evolving logic of participant observation, educational ethnography and other case studies. In L. Shulman (Ed.), *Review of research in education.* Chicago: Peacock Press, 1979.

Stake, R. E. The case study method in social inquiry. *Educational Researcher,* Feb. 1978, 5-8.

Stake, R. E., et al. *Evaluating the arts in education: A responsive approach.* Columbus, Ohio: Charles E. Merrill Publishing, 1975.

Willems, R., & Raush, H. L. (Eds.). *Naturalistic viewpoints in psychological research.* New York: Holt, Rinehart and Winston, 1968.

. . . Why do them

Guba, E. G. Toward a methodology of naturalistic inquiry in educational evaluation. *CSE Monograph Series in Evaluation, No. 8.* Los Angeles: Center for the Study of Evaluation, UCLA Graduate School of Education, 1978.

Stenhouse, L. *An introduction to curriculum research and development.* London: Heinemann Educational Books, 1975.

. . . Some examples

Jackson, P. *Life in classrooms.* New York: Holt, Rinehart, & Winston, 1968.

Stake, B. E. PLATO and fourth grade mathematics. *Journal of Research on Children's Mathematics,* 1978, *2*(2).

Tikunoff, W., Berliner, D. C., & Rist, R. C. *An ethnographic study of the forty classrooms of the beginning teachers evaluation study: A known sample* (Technical Report #75-10-10-5). San Francisco: Far West Regional Laboratory, October, 1975.

Chapter 2

An Outline of an Implementation Report

This chapter contains an outline of what is usually discussed in a report about program implementation. If you are a *formative* evaluator, you might take the term *report* loosely and use the information in this chapter as a checklist of possible topics you could address. If you are a *summative* evaluator, you will probably take the term *report* more seriously, allowing part of the outline to suggest the content and form of the written document you produce.

Whether you are a formative or a summative evaluator, if you need to prepare a detailed implementation report, you might simply name each section according to the headings listed in this chapter, and answer the questions under each heading in as much detail as is necessary to your evaluation role and level of effort. This exercise will give you a working draft of the report. Primarily, consider the outline provided here as a kind of cookbook, perhaps dropping or adding questions as you see fit, or perhaps amplifying some of the original questions to make them more appropriate to your setting, or perhaps changing their order.

In addition to choosing *what* to describe about the program, you will need to decide which portions of your description must be supported by corroborating evidence. The necessity to collect backup data to underlie your description of some program features will, of course, be primarily a function of the setting of *your* evaluation. But there are program features which, because of their complexity, controversial nature, or critical weight within programs, usually require backup data regardless of the context. To remind you that your description of certain features may meet skepticism, the symbol **√DATA** appears in the outline next to questions whose answers could require accompanying evidence.

The outline in this chapter will yield a report describing program implementation *only*. In most evaluations, implementation issues comprise only one facet of a more elaborate enterprise concerned with the design of the evaluation, the intended outcomes of the program, the measures used to assess achievement of those outcomes, and the results these measures produced. If this description of an extended evaluation responsibility matches your task, then information from the outline here will need to be incorporated into a larger report discussing other aspects of the program and its evaluation. If, in fact, the evaluation compares the effects of two different programs considered equally important by your audience, then you should prepare an implementation report to describe them both.

The headings and questions in this chapter are organized according to the five major sections of an implementation report:

1. A summary which gives the reader a quick synopsis of the report.

2. A description of the *context* in which the program has been implemented, focusing mainly upon the setting, administrative arrangements, personnel, and resources involved.

3. A description of the point of view from which implementation has been examined. This section can have one of two characters:

   a. It can describe the program's most critical features as *prescribed* by a program plan, a theory or teaching model, or someone's predictions about what will make the program succeed or fail.

   b. It can explain the responsive/naturalistic evaluator's choice to *not* use a prescription to guide her examination of the program.

4. A description of the implementation evaluation itself—the choice of measures, the range of program activities examined, the sites examined, etc. This section also includes a rationale for choosing the data sources listed.

5. Results of implementation backup measures and discussion of program implementation. This section can either:

   a. Describe the extent to which the program as implemented fit the one that was planned or prescribed by a plan, theory, or teaching model.

   b. Describe implementation independent of underlying intent. This description, usually gathered using a responsive/naturalistic method, reflects a decision that the evaluator describe what she discovered rather than compare program events with underlying points of view.

   In either case, this section describes what has been found, noting variations in the program across sites or time. The report concludes with an interpretation of the results and suggestions for further program development or evaluation.

Report Section I. Summary

The summary is a brief overview of the report, explaining *why* a description of implementation has been undertaken and listing the major conclusions and recommendations to be found in Section 5. Since the summary is designed for people who are too busy to read the full report, it should be limited to one or two pages. Although the summary is placed *first* in the report, it is the *last* section to be written.

Typical Content of the Summary Section

- What is the *name* of the program whose implementation has been measured?
- Why has the implementation evaluation been conducted?
- Is the evaluation intended to be formative or summative?
- What are the major findings and recommendations of the implementation evaluation?

Report Section II. Background and Context of the Program

This section sets the program in context. It describes how the program was initiated, what it was supposed to do, and the resources available. The amount of information presented will depend upon the audiences for whom the report has been prepared. If the audience has *no knowledge* of the program, the program must be fully described. If, on the other hand, the implementation report is mainly intended for internal use and its readers are likely to be familiar with the program, this section can be brief and set down information "for the record." Regardless of the audience, if your report will be *written,* it might become the sole lasting record of the program's implementation. In this case, the context section should contain considerable data.

If your program's setting includes many different schools or districts, it may not be practical to cover the questions below separately for each school or district. Instead, for each question indicate *similarities and differences* among schools or districts or the range represented, or the most typical pattern that occurred.

Typical Content of Background Section

A. The program's setting

- Where has the program been implemented? What sort of locales? What states, regions, communities, or neighborhoods have program participants come from?
- How many and what sorts of people does the program affect? What are the characteristics of the population affected; for example, its density, trends of influx and exit, ethnic grouping, mobility rate, birth and divorce rates, percentage of young and aged? √DATA

- What are the economic characteristics of the setting? What are the major occupations of people in the locale? What is the unemployment rate or trend? **VDATA** What proportion of families are receiving welfare assistance? **VDATA**
- What power or interest groups affect events in the locale? For example, is there a segment of the community which is particularly powerful, perhaps in political terms or in the manner in which they express their opinions?
- What are the major characteristics of the school system or the state, district, or single school in which the program took place? What grade levels are served? How many pupils are in the system? How many schools or classrooms are there? What type? What is the average teacher-pupil ratio? Are there any significant trends in school system enrollments, attendance, withdrawals, or transfers? **VDATA**
- What is the financial status of the school system? What is the per pupil cost of education? **VDATA** What is the system's financial history?
- What issues of accountability affect the program? For example, are there certain areas for which dollar amounts must be spent and for which the program is accountable? Are there program elements which staff *must* implement, such as delivery of particular program services to children in an area of special education?

B. The origins of the program

- How did the program get started? Was a formal or informal *needs assessment*[13] conducted, and if so, what were the results? **VDATA**
- What was the starting point for the needs assessment? Did the state, district, or school determine the needs? Were needs determined by a committee of local citizens or school officials? Who were they? **VDATA** Are needs determined by prominent or vocal individuals or groups? Who? **VDATA**
- How were the *needs of pupils* identified? Through a survey to identify children with particular problems? What did it conclude? **VDATA** Through standardized testing? What were the results? **VDATA** Through recognition of disturbing events such as a high school dropout rate, delinquency, literacy, crime rate, school attendance, or academic achievement levels? Through training needs established by college admissions requirements or suggested by needs of employers?
- Were the opinions of parents, teachers, counselors, community, or pupils solicited. What were these opinions? **VDATA**
- What *specific* needs guided the direction of the program? What priorities were determined? How? **VDATA** How were these needs translated into goals or objectives for the program?

C. Goals of the program

- What was the program designed to accomplish?
- What goals or objectives were set? How were they set and by whom? **VDATA** For example, did program staff use the established needs or priorities as the basis to develop objectives? Did staff select objectives from available collections to meet the established priorities? Were these goals and

---

13. Needs assessment is a process by which the *goals* of an organization, such as a school, are first selected or generated and then assigned priorities. This process, which seeks to determine the needs of the organization, usually asks members of its constituency – say, the community – to express opinions.

objectives offered to other members of the school or community for review to achieve consensus on their appropriateness? A listing of goals and objectives underlying the program might be attached to this section of the report.

D. Historical background

- Did the program exist prior to the time period covered in the present report? When did it originate? Was it known by the same title as the present program? What evidence of previous success or failure can be provided? **√DATA**
- If the program is a modification of a previously existing program, have the characteristics of the participants changed? Have the characteristics of the program changed?
- Whose idea was it to implement this particular form of program? How did the idea develop to the point of a completed program? Who motivated the program development? Who designed, developed, or chose it? By what authority?
- Were problems encountered in gaining acceptance of the program by parents or by the community? How were these solved so that the program could be introduced? For example, did the school or district hold meetings to share information about the program with the community and to enlist their cooperation and support?

E. The program's target group

- For what age, grade level, and ability level of students is the program appropriate?
- How many participants have been served by the particular program during the evaluation?
- On what basis have participants (students, classrooms, schools, districts) been selected for the program? **√DATA** For example, were students with high need in the particular content area assigned to the program? If so, how was high need determined? Are the proper people receiving the program's services? **√DATA** Are participants to remain in the program for its duration? If not, what criteria determine the time of their entrance or exit? **√DATA**
- In what *aggregate* are people participating in the program? In other words, is it more appropriate to talk about participants in terms of districts, schools, classrooms, or individuals?
- In what ways are participants grouped? For instance, do students take part in the program en masse as members of classrooms or smaller subgroups? How many students per class or group? **√DATA** Do classrooms differ in significant ways? For example, are some open versus traditional groupings used? **√DATA** Are participating schools different in any way? **√DATA** In size? In student body composition? Do parochial or church schools or private schools participate as well as public schools? If participants are teachers or administrators, what differences in background, qualifications, or experience characterize the group? **√DATA**

F. Program personnel

- What *kinds* and *numbers* of personnel took part in the program? **√DATA** How best can their *roles* be described? For example, as instructional versus non-instructional staff; as administrative, instructional, or support staff? The answer to this question may demand a list of job descriptions. For example, "The program provided 20 full time teacher aides who assisted the teachers with non-instructional or clerical tasks in the classrooms such as role call, preparation of snacks, recess supervision, and clean-up." An organizational chart might also convey the staffing pattern of the program.

- Are staff members required to have special backgrounds or credentials? Do they? **√DATA** What procedures were used for selecting the staff?
- Were any of these staff to receive training in connection with the program? Did they? **√DATA**
- What special problems have been dealt with in recruiting or maintaining the staff? For example, if aides or teachers need special training to participate in the program, has official release time been given for this training? Does training occur in the evenings or weekends thereby causing dropoff in staff support?
- How much time do people in each staff role devote to responsibilities connected with the program?
- As the program has evolved, have certain job roles dropped out? Were some roles changed or others added? Why?
- How do *parents* participate in the program? Are they actively involved in the classroom? Do they work as advisors, counselors, mentors, instructors? How many—and which—parents have participated? **√DATA**
- Is parental permission required for students to participate in program activities? Has it been obtained? **√DATA** How? **√DATA**
- If parents serve as advisors, what percent of parents actually advise? Are these parents typical of the whole school-parent group? **√DATA**

G. Administrative arrangements

- Are the administrative arrangements that have been made major components of the program themselves, or does administration merely *support* a program whose main focus is instructional?
- How is the program administered? What offices or roles have been created or expanded? Does this represent a departure from the usual practice?
- What people fill chief administrative positions? Has the administrative staffing of the program remained fairly stable throughout, or has there been job shifting? Why, or why not?

H. Budget

- What has been the total cost of implementing this program? **√DATA** What are the major cost items?
- From what sources have program funds been obtained?
- What period of time is covered by these funds? What proportion of program costs are paid by the district, by grants from the Federal or State government, or by foundations? **√DATA** What portion of program costs consists of monies that would have been spent anyway? **√DATA** What proportion of monies is made up of funds specifically granted for operating the program? **√DATA**
- If the program has run for several years or several funding periods, what changes in sources of funds and cost trends have occurred?
- Of the cost of the program, what portion could be called *start-up* and what portion could be called *continuation* costs? Give rough dollar estimates. A start-up cost is money and time spent on *development* of materials, planning, etc., things that occur only once in the life of a program. Continuation costs are expenditures needed to keep the program running once it is off the ground. Continuation costs, for example, are reflected in the annual salaries of the teachers hired especially for the program.
- Depending upon the figures you have available to you, what breakdown by broad categories and amounts can you show of the total cost of the program? **√DATA** For example, what are the costs of acquiring, maintaining, and operating the program plan? What has been the cost of developing materials?

Of training the staff? Of providing support services? How much is it costing to disseminate information about the program? What were the salaries of various personnel categories?

- What is the per pupil cost of the program? **√DATA** What formula has been used for computing this figure?[14]
- How does the per pupil cost of the program compare with per pupil cost at the various sites if the program had not been initiated? **√DATA**
- Where can the reader obtain more detailed budget information?

Note for Sections II, III, and IV of the Implementation Report

If your evaluation is comparing the program with a *control,* the program received by control groups will need to be described as well—and in as much detail as possible. The extent of this description will depend on your audience's intentions regarding the control group's program. If the program is a viable alternative for adoption in lieu of or in addition to the program under scrutiny, then the description of the implementation of the control program should be as extensively and carefully treated as the description of the program under scrutiny. If the control program is *not* in contention for possible adoption, then you will need to describe only those aspects of the control program which might most strongly affect the outcomes of that program. These program features include *contextual information* such as community demographic characteristics, student ability, and ethnicity, and *critical program activities* in which they engaged such as materials used and length of time spent on instruction. If the control students received *no program* aimed at objectives similar to the program under scrutiny, then you should still include a description of what the control students did while the program students were engaged in their program.

**Report Section III. General Description of the
Critical Features of the Program as
Planned—Materials and Activities**

This section presents a general overview of the program, leaving specific detail to the discussion of results in Section V.

If you wish to present a *detailed* prescription of program implementation, then use the outline of Section V as a source of suggested topics. Consider, as well, organizing the program prescription into a table or list as described on pages 59 and 60.

If your look at implementation is responsive and naturalistic, explain that you have chosen to omit this section.

---

14. A useful figure for describing cost per pupil results from dividing all costs paid out of program funds by the number of pupils who attended the program *on what you have defined as a regular basis.* This number eliminates excessive absentees from the total number of students. You might also calculate a per pupil cost based only on *continuation* costs. In order to do this, subtract the start-up costs from the total program expenditure before dividing by the number of pupils.

Typical Content of Planned Critical Program Features Section

A. **Major planned program characteristics**

- If a program plan has directed your implementation study, what does it say the program is *supposed to* look like? How much variation does it allow? This description boils down essentially to an outline of the major materials to be used, the activities engaged in, the person responsible for implementing each program feature, and the target participants in each activity. It might also include a projection of the amount of progress expected to be made in each activity by a certain time.
- If a theory, philosophical stance, model of schooling, or expert opinion has directed the implementation study, what program features have these directed you to examine? Why?
- Does the plan or theory underlying your implementation study stipulate that something it considers detrimental be *absent* from the program? What and why?
- What is the *rationale* underlying the program? That is, why do the program's planners feel that the various program materials and activities they have selected will lead to the achievement of program goals?
- How highly prescribed is program implementation? How much is the program allowed to vary from site to site or from time to time?

B. **Plans for program review and renewal**

- What provisions have been made for periodic review of the program? How often should it occur? Are reviews done internally or do they include outside assistance? What techniques are used to monitor and/or modify program operations on a day-to-day basis?
- What planning or problem solving meetings occur to help remedy the program problems or to share program successes? What decisions are made on the basis of review and/or information on program weaknesses or strengths?

Report Section IV. Description of the Implementation Evaluation: Selection of Program Characteristics To Examine and Choice of Implementation Measures

This section consists of a discussion of the program activities you selected for examination and measures chosen to examine them.

.Typical Content of Description of Implementation Evaluation

A. **Focus of the implementation evaluation**

- Is measurement primarily conducted for formative or summative purposes? That is, will your information feed back to the staff for the purpose of program improvement, or will the implementation study comprise a summarization of the program?
- Who are the audiences of your report? The program staff? Parents? Community? School board? State or federal agencies?
- Is the implementation study being undertaken from the point of view of assessing the match between the program as implemented and the program as

planned? For examining the implementation of a theory or point of view? Or is the evaluation responsive/naturalistic, aiming to describe what is happening in lieu of pre-planning? Why has this particular point of view been taken?

- What is the context of your implementation study? Are there restrictions, constraints of time or money, or other limitations influencing the course and direction of your study? Are there particular issues that you have decided not to address? Did you make this decision alone or in consultation with the program staff?

- *Which* critical program characteristics—materials and activities—discussed in Section 3 have you chosen to concentrate on in assembling your description? Why? For instance, were some activities selected because of their sheer critical weight to the program? If so, how was critical weight determined? Did a program activity reflect an important notion in a theory of teaching or educational point of view? Was it described as being important by program staff or others? Was critical value determined, in part or in whole, by frequency of citation in a program plan, by its budgetary and other resource allocation? Was critical weight established, in part or in whole, by issues of accountability?

- If your report will not attempt to compare actual with planned program occurrence, how have you decided which activities to describe? Alone or in consultation with program staff and others?

- Does your selection of program features to examine seem to be representative of the total program? What provisions have you made to detect or allow for program variations across sites or over time?

- For which aspects of your description have you decided to collect backup data? Why? For which aspects *might* you have chosen to collect such data but will not? Why?

B. Range of measures and data collection

- What types of instruments have you chosen to use as your source of data? Will you rely on informal information gathering methods such as casual observations or conversations with program staff? Or formal methods such as systematic observation or questionnaires? Are you using some combination of these types?

- How have instruments been selected? Have you found ready-made ones to copy or purchase? From whom and on what basis?

- If instruments have been developed, who undertook the task? What were their time and budget constraints? What are their qualifications for developing measures? **√DATA** How did they go about developing the measures?

- What limitations or deficiencies are there in the instruments used?

- Were checks made on instrument validity, reliability, and appropriateness to the setting? **√DATA**

- What data collection procedures were used? What was the schedule for the collection of implementation information? And who collected it? A schedule is often well presented by a table.

- What training was provided and what precautions were taken to ensure appropriate use of instruments? **√DATA**

- Were instruments—questionnaires, interviews—administered to everyone or to a representative group? Who? And how were they chosen? **√DATA** In other words, what sampling plan did you use? (see page 60.)

- What limitations or deficiencies were there in the sampling or scheduling used for measuring implementation?

Report Section V. Results of Measures and Discussion of Program Implementation

Typical Content

A. Overview and general considerations

- What is the period of time covered by your report? How much of the entire program does it cover?
- In general, does the program that has been delivered resemble the one that was intended? Has the program been implemented at every site as planned and as the audience expected? If not, what has happened? Have some components been dropped or modified? Are all materials available? Have they been used? Has the program been delivered to the audience for whom it was planned? Have crucial activities in fact occurred?
- How is the community being informed about your findings? For example, has information been provided through news releases, television coverage, open meetings?

B. Specific findings and conclusions

For *each set of materials* your evaluation has examined, answer the following questions:

- Do the materials seem to fit the program's objectives? VDATA
- What materials does the program actually use and how? VDATA Which have been purchased, and which produced in-house?
- If special materials have been developed or adapted for the program, who did it? When? Over the summer? After school? Were program funds provided? If readers are interested in obtaining or duplicating these materials, from what sources are they available?
- If materials have been custom-produced, have developers been able to provide the quantity needed in the time allotted and with the funds available? VDATA
- Are the materials generally durable or must they be replaced fairly often, for example, more than once every two years? What percent of the total materials purchased must be replaced? VDATA How often? VDATA
- Where would one find available for examination a complete set of the materials developed in-house?
- If commercially produced materials have been purchased, which ones and how many? VDATA For what grade level? VDATA For what groups? VDATA
- Are purchased materials durable or must they be replaced fairly often? VDATA How often? VDATA
- Where can a complete set of the purchased materials be examined? For example, are they available for inspection in the school or district or only from the publisher or developer?
- What degree of structure, sequencing, and adaptation to the needs of individual participants is evident in the materials? VDATA
- Do you have evidence that the materials were interesting or stimulating to students and instructors? VDATA
- *Which materials and facilities have been most often used, fairly often used, seldom used, never used?* VDATA
- What program settings outside the classroom have been used—such as playground, gym, field trip locale? What percent of program time was spent at each place? VDATA
- What other resources—physical facilities, transportation—have been used to

support the program, and who provided them? For example, are special facilities provided by community groups such as businessmen? Is district transportation available for field trips?

For *each different activity* which the program has encompassed, answer the following questions:

- Do the activities seem to fit the program's objectives?
- In what activities have participants in the program, such as students, taken part? To what extent—often, fairly often, seldom, never? **VDATA** Which staff members direct the activities? A good way to convey this information is to add a sixth column to the program objectives/activities table on page 59. In this column, you might enter estimates of the degree of actual implementation.
- Have special measures been taken to motivate students to participate in program activities? Do these methods seem to work? **VDATA**
- What do the critical activities comprising the program look like in practice? **VDATA** Use actual vignettes describing typical classroom incidents. Are there available informal comments or narrative summaries which you can copy or quote which illustrate the findings indicated by your other data? Are there photographs? Or sketches? Student or teacher products? Parent letters? Student essays or transcripts of informal observations? Were testimonials about the program which you have been able to collect solicited or voluntary?
- Do you have evidence that the activities are interesting to teachers and students?
- How much interpersonal instructional contact do the activities give to students? **VDATA** Does this vary greatly according to student characteristics?
- What is included in a typical day's or week's schedule of activity for the children or others involved in the program? **VDATA** You might include here a typical schedule to show *how much time* is devoted to the particular activities, the time of day when these occur, and the sequence in which participants experience them.
- How are pupils grouped for various program activities? **VDATA**
- What are the actual teacher-pupil ratios (or aide-pupil, adult-pupil, or other role ratios) in each of these groupings? **VDATA** Explain what is meant by such terms as "large group" or "small group."
- What specific and routine procedures which can be described in extreme detail, if any, do teachers or other program implementors follow? **VDATA** Do teachers, for instance, typically make to students certain sorts of reinforcing comments which can be described verbatim? Do teachers typically require certain minimum levels of behavior from students—speaking English a certain percent of time in class, or requiring students to read aloud a certain number of pages or amount of time per day?
- What amount and kinds of practice, review, and quizzes are provided for students in the program? **VDATA** Include here descriptions of the content of such activities, their frequency, and the methods used.
- How do pupils or others receive feedback about their individual progress? **VDATA** Through verbal or written critiques of their work, for example, or explanation of scores from regular classroom quizzes?
- How are parents informed about their children's progress? **VDATA** For example, have parent-teacher conferences been held? How frequently? **VDATA** Have parents been invited to observe their children in class? **VDATA** To what extent has parental advice been sought in planning each child's activities? **VDATA**

- If problems with parents or the community have affected the program, what steps, if any, have been taken to remedy them?
- What special provisions have been made for motivating pupils or others? **VDATA** Were these a planned part of the program?
- How much variation has there been in the program from site to site and from time to time? **VDATA** How much of this represents variation that was planned and how much variation that was unexpected?
- What are the important differences in the activities and methods used by the comparison group and the activities and methods used with the program group?
- What does the control or comparison group look like? Are students grouped in the same way as program students? What is the average, median, or mean age of students in the control group? **VDATA** What grade levels do they comprise? **VDATA** What is their socio-economic level?
- What characteristics of the control students can be pointed out which show that they are essentially the same type of students as the program students? **VDATA** Pay particular attention to the student features that have been used as criteria for selection of program students, for instance, IQ or musical ability.
- What characteristics of the control group make them *different* from those of the program group? **VDATA** For example, do they differ in level of entry skills or in geographical location?
- If the control group is a non-randomized, non-equivalent one, can you confidently make the following statement: "Although students were not randomly assigned to the control and program groups, our data show them to be so alike in critical features related to the program that they might as well have been randomly distributed to groups"? Why or why not? **VDATA**
- What materials, personnel, and facilities used by the control group are similar to those in the program described in this report? **VDATA** For example, do the two groups use the same reading series? Do both have aides? Do they use the same classroom facilities? Do they make the same field trips? Are teachers similarly trained? Do they spend about the same amount of time on instruction in the relevant subject matter areas? **VDATA**
- How has dropout and influx of the control group compared with that of the program group? How do they compare with the dropout and influx rate typical of the control group's own school or district?
- Does the staff feel that the program as it appears could be improved were it to be modified or run for a longer period of time? Is there evidence in your data to support their point of view? What conclusions about quality or extent of program implementation have you been able to draw from your examination of the program?

Chapter 3

Measuring Program Implementation

Chapter 1 listed reasons for including an accurate program description in your evaluation report. These reasons included the need to set down a concrete description of the program that could be used for its replication, to provide a basis for making conjectures about relationships between implementation and program effects, and to collect accountability evidence demonstrating that the program staff delivered the service they promised. The *summative* evaluator will be concerned about documenting a program's implementation for one or more of these purposes. The *formative* evaluator, on the other hand, will primarily be concerned about tracking changes in a program's implementation, keeping a record of the program's developmental history, and giving feedback to the program staff about bugs, flaws, and successes in the process of program installation.

Looking through Chapter 2 probably helped you to decide which characteristics of the program need describing. At some point in your thinking about program implementation, you will make a related decision about which of these descriptions need substantiating; that is, which parts of your report need to be backed up by data which you collect.

If you are a summative evaluator, the simplest way to describe program activities, materials, and administration—but unfortunately the least adequate for most purposes—is to use an existing description of the program (i.e., the plan or proposal) to double as your program implementation report. If you are severely pressed by time and other constraints, and if a plan exists, you *may* get by with this. But if you or a member of your staff have time to spend on actually *measuring* implementation, then your description of the program will be richer and subsequently more useful and credible. If you are a formative evaluator whose job is to report about what is going on at the program sites, you cannot help but become involved in some implementation measurements. For those who will do the measuring, this chapter presents several methods that might help you obtain backup data for your report.

When Do You Need Backup Data?

You might need to describe program implementation for people who are at some *distance* from the program, either in terms of location or familiarity. These people will base their opinions about the program's form and quality on what they read in your description. You might therefore need to provide backup data to verify its accuracy.

If the description you produce is for people *close* to the program and familiar with it, then you can rely on the audience's detailed knowledge of the program in operation—at least in their own setting. In such a case, you may want to focus your data collection on the extent to which the program's implementation at one site is representative of its implementation at other sites. The credibility of your report for people close to the program will, of course, depend on how well your description of the program matches what they see. If you feel that your report of overall program implementation diverges considerably from the experiences of the program's administration or of participants at any one site, then you may need to collect good, hard backup data.

Examples of more specific circumstances calling for backup data are:

- Summative evaluations which constitute research studies addressed to the educational community at large
- Evaluations aimed at providing new information for a situation where there is likely to be controversy
- Evaluations calling for program implementation descriptions so detailed that they characterize program activity at the level of teacher or student behaviors
- Descriptions of programs that may be used as a basis for adopting or adapting the program in other settings
- Descriptions of programs which have varied considerably from site to site or from time to time

How you use backup data will be determined in part by which of the approaches to describing the program you adopt:

1. Using the program plan as a baseline and examining how well the program as implemented fits the plan.
2. Using a theory or model to decide the features that should be present in the program. In this case you will probably consult research literature or prescriptions of various philosophical or psychological points of view for guidance in what to look for. In both this and the plan-based approaches, backup data will be necessary to permit people to judge

how closely the actual program fits what was planned. Such data could also help you document your discovery of program features that were not planned.

3. Following no particular prescription and instead taking a responsive/ naturalistic stance regarding the program. In this situation you will attempt to enter the program sites with no initial preconceptions or assumptions about what the program should look like.

If you assume either of the first two points of view concerning focus and use of data, your final report will describe the fit of the program to the prescription you have chosen to use. In the third situation, your final report will simply describe the program that you found, noting, of course, variability from site to site.

Methods of Data Collection

This book helps you to use three prevalent and practical approaches to collecting backup data. Use of any one does *not* exclude use of the others. Which method or combination of methods you select will primarily be a function of the overall purpose of the evaluation, the audiences involved, and their information needs. In short, selection of data collection methods depends on the extent to which your report must provide richness of data to be considered accurate and credible from the standpoint of your audiences.

Method 1. Examine the Records Kept Over the Course of the Program

These might include sign-in sheets for materials, library loan records, individual student assignment cards, teachers' logs of activities in the classroom. In a program where extensive records are kept as a matter of course, you may be able to extract from them a substantial part of the data you need to determine what activities occurred, what materials were used, and how and with whom activities took place and materials were used. This method will yield credible evaluation information because it provides evidence of program events accumulated *as they occurred* rather than reconstructed later. The major drawback of existing records is that abstracting information from them can be time consuming. Then again, records kept over the course of the program will probably not meet all your data collection requirements. If it looks as though the existing records are inadequate, you have two alternatives. The best one is to set up *your own record-keeping system,* assuming, of course, that you have arrived on the scene in time to do this. A weaker alternative is to gather *recollected* versions of program records from participants. Should you do this, point out in your report the extent to which this information has been corroborated by more formal records or results from other measures.

Method 2. Conduct Observations

Have one or more observers make periodic visits to program sites and record their observations, either freely or according to a pre-determined list of activities. On-site observation, though it consumes a fair amount of time and effort, has high credibility because the observer views program events as they occur. You can enhance that credibility by demonstrating that the data from the observations are reliable, that is, consistent across different observers and over time.

Method 3. Use Self-Report Measures

Have program personnel and participants—teachers, aides, parents, administrators and in some cases, students—give you descriptions of what program activities look like. It makes sense, of course, to turn for information about a program to the people who worked with it. You might choose to *interview* people or give them *questionnaires.* If collecting information from *everyone* who experienced the program will take too much effort and time, then ask for descriptions of activities from *a sample* of people within each role group.

Since different groups of participants in a program might have divergent perceptions, you may want to gather self-report information, probably on a sample basis, from teachers, administrators, parents, and students and compare the information provided by different groups to see if you get a consistent, or reliable, set of pictures about the program.

Be aware that *self-report* measures could have credibility problems depending on the situation. Usually people close to the program will find such information to be credible. People far from the program—for instance, at the funding agency—are less likely to trust self-report information from the staff. First of all, there is the possibility that people providing you with information have a vested interest in making the program look good. Then again, even when intentional bias is unlikely, self-report descriptions of a program are at best second-hand accounts of what transpired—the *evaluator* tells the *audience* what people *say they did.* Thirdly, self-report information often consists of recollections after-the-fact of peoples' *own* behavior. Accounts of what people remember having done themselves are usually not as credible as descriptions by others who actually *saw* what they did.

Because of their credibility problems and the detail with which program implementation usually needs to be described, self-report instruments are more often used to verify or to check on the *consistency* across sites of a program description arrived at by more direct means. Only when the evaluator's resources are too limited to permit collection of close-up data do self-report measures constitute the primary source of implementation information.

To help you think about your own situation, Table 2, pages 54 and 55, summarizes the advantages and disadvantages of each of the three methods of data collection. Chapters 4, 5, and 6 describe the three data collection methods in greater detail.

Chapter 4 provides assistance in using records to assess program implementation. It talks about setting up a record-keeping system and checking program records that are already in existence. Chapter 5 deals with classroom observations. It describes methods for conducting both informal and systematic observations. The section on systematic observations presents several alternative schemes for coding information, one of which should fit your situation. Chapter 6 describes ways of using self-report instruments with staff members, parents, students, etc. It describes step-by-step procedures for constructing and administering *questionnaires,* and conducting *interviews.* To help you assess the quality of the measures you produce, Chapter 7 briefly discusses validity and reliability—the accuracy and consistency—of implementation measurement methods.

If it is important that you describe a program feature accurately, and/or if your audience might be skeptical, then you should try to assemble *converging* data. This requires using *multiple measures and data collection methods* and gathering data from different participants at different sites. For example, if you were evaluating a program based on individualization, you might want to document the extent to which instruction really is determined according to individual needs. To assure enough evidence, you could collect different kinds of data. Maybe you would *interview* students at the various program sites about the sequence and pacing of their lessons and the extent to which instruction occurs in groups. To corroborate what you find through student interviews, you could examine the teachers' *record-keeping* systems. In an individualized program it is likely that teachers would maintain charts or prescription forms tracking individual student progress. Finally, you might conduct a few *observations* or spot checks, watching typical classes in session to estimate the amount of individual instruction and progress-monitoring per student—both within and across sites. Three sources of information—interviews, examination of records, and classroom observation—could then be reported, each supporting or qualifying the findings of another.

Where To Look For Already Existing Measures

Before you involve yourself in the onerous business of designing your own implementation measure, you might take a look at instruments already available. Some measures, mainly observation schedules and questionnaires, have been developed which can be used to describe general charac-

TABLE 2

Method 1: Examine Records.

Records are systematic accounts of regular occurrences consisting of such things as attendance and enrollment reports, sign-in sheets, library checkout records, permission slips, counselor files, teacher logs, individual student assignment cards, etc.

Method 2: Conduct Observations.

Observations require that one or more observers devote all their attention to the behavior of an individual or group within a natural setting and for a prescribed time period. In some cases, an observer may be given detailed guidelines about who or what to observe, when and how long to observe, and the method of recording the information. An instrument to record this kind of information would likely be formatted as a questionnaire or tally sheet. An observer may also be sent into a classroom with less restrictive instructions, i.e., without detailed guidelines, and simply asked to write a responsive/naturalistic account of events which occurred within the prescribed time period.

Method 3: Use Self-Report Measures.

Questionnaires are instruments that present information to a respondent in writing or through the use of pictures and then require a written response—a check, a circle, a word, a sentence, or several sentences.

Interviews involve a face-to-face meeting between two (or more) persons in which a respondent answers questions posed by an interviewer. The questions may be predetermined, but the interviewer is free to pursue interesting responses. The respondent's answers are usually recorded in some way by the interviewer during the interview, but a summary of the responses is generally completed afterwards.

Methods for Collecting Backup Data

Advantages	Disadvantages
• Records kept for purposes other than the program evaluation can be a source of data gathered without additional demands on people's time and energies. • Records are often viewed as objective and therefore credible. • Records set down events at the time of occurrence rather than in retrospect. This also increases credibility.	• Records may be incomplete. • The process of examining them and extracting relevant information can be time-consuming. • There may be ethical or legal constraints involved in your examination of certain kinds of records —counselor files for example. • Asking people to keep records specifically for the program evaluation may be seen as burdensome.
• Observations can be highly credible when seen as the report of what actually took place presented by disinterested outsider(s). • Observers provide a point of view different from that of people most closely connected with the program.	• The presence of observers may alter what takes place. • Time is needed to develop the observation instrument and train observers if the observation is highly prescribed. • It is necessary to locate credible observers if the observation is not carefully controlled. • Time is needed to conduct sufficient numbers of observations. • There are usually scheduling problems.
• Questionnaires provide the answers to a variety of questions. • They can be answered anonymously. • They allow the respondent time to think before responding. • They can be given to many people, at distant sites, simultaneously. • They can be mailed. • They impose uniformity on the information obtained by asking all respondents the same things, e.g., asking teachers to supply the names of all math games used in class throughout the semester.	• They do not provide the flexibility of interviews. • People are often better able to express themselves orally than in writing. • Persuading people to complete and return questionnaires is sometimes difficult.
• Interviews can be used to obtain information from people who cannot read and from non-native speakers who might have difficulties with the wording of written questions. • Interviews permit flexibility. They allow the interviewer to pursue unanticipated lines of inquiry.	• Interviewing is time-consuming. • Sometimes the interviewer can unduly influence the responses of the interviewee.

teristics of groups, classrooms, and other educational units. Titles of these instruments often mention:

- School or classroom climate
- Patterns of interaction and verbal communication
- Characteristics of the environment

If you wish to explore some of these, check these anthologies:

Borich, G. D., & Madden, S. K. *Evaluating classroom instruction: A sourcebook of instruments.* Menlo Park, CA: Addison-Wesley Publishing, 1977.

This sourcebook contains a comprehensive review of instruments for evaluating instruction and describing classroom activities. It lists 171 instruments, describes each along with its availability, reliability, validity, norms, if any, and procedures for administration and scoring. Each is also briefly reviewed, and sample items are provided. Only measures which have been empirically validated appear in the sourcebook. The instruments are cross-classified according to what the instrument describes (teacher, pupil, or classroom) and who provides the information (the teacher, the pupil, an observer).

Boyer, E. G., Simon, A., & Karafin, G. R. (Eds.). *Measures of maturation.* Philadelphia: Research for Better Schools, Humanizing Learning Program.

This is a three-volume anthology of 73 early childhood observation systems. Most of these systems were developed for research purposes, but some can be used for program evaluation.

The 73 systems are classified according to:

- The kinds of behavior that can be observed (individual actions and social contacts of various types)
- The attributes of the physical environment
- The nature and uses of the data and the manner in which it is collected
- The appropriate age range and other characteristics of those observed

Each system is described in detail.

Simon, A., & Boyer, E. G. *Mirrors for behavior: An anthology of classroom observation instruments.* Philadelphia: Research for Better Schools, Center for the Study of Teaching, 1974.

This collection provides abstracts of 99 classroom observation systems. Each abstract contains information on the subjects of the observation, the setting, the methods of collecting the data, the type of behavior that is recorded, and the ways in which the data can be used. In addition, an extensive bibliography directs the reader to further information on these systems and how they have been used by others.

An earlier edition of this work (1967) provides detailed descriptions of twenty-six of these systems.

Price, J. L. *Handbook of organizational measurement.* New York: Heath, 1972.

This handbook lists and classifies measures which describe various features of organizations. The measures are applicable, but not limited to, schools and school districts. The instruments are classified according to organizational characteristics, e.g., communication, complexity, innovation, centralization. The text defines each characteristic and its measurement. Then it describes and evaluates instruments relevant to the characteristic, mentioning validity and reliability data, sources from which the measure can be obtained, and references for additional reading.

The Bases of a Good Plan For Constructing
Your Own Measures

Regardless of which or how many data collection methods you choose, your information gathering will be built on three important bases. These should be set up in advance:

1. A list of the activities, materials and administrative procedures on which you will focus
2. A sampling strategy—a list of which sites you will examine, who will be contacted, talked with and/or observed, as well as when and how often
3. A plan for data summary and analysis

Constructing a List of Program Characteristics

A thoughtful look through the program's plan or proposal, a talk with staff and planners, your own thinking about what the program should look like—perhaps based on its underlying theory or philosophy—and careful consideration of the implementation questions in Chapter 2 should help you arrive at a *list of the program materials, activities or administrative procedures* whose implementation you want to track. Make sure that the program features you list are detailed and exhaustive of those considered—by the staff, planners, and other audiences—to be crucial to the program. *Detailed* means the list should include a prescription of the *frequency* or *duration* of activities and of their *form* (who, how, where) that is specific enough to allow you to picture each activity in your mind's eye.

If you are looking at a plan or proposal, then critical features will often be those *most frequently cited* and those to which the *largest part of the budget* and other resources have been allotted. For example, if large sets of curriculum materials were purchased for the program, then one critical part of the program implementation is the proper use of these materials.

If your work with the program will be *formative,* then you should attend to parts of the program that are likely to need revision or cause problems. Try to *visit* one or more sites in which the program is operating and observe the environment, the materials, the people, and the activities before you consider your list of program features complete. This way, you will be able to envision the actual program situation when you construct implementation instruments.

The program characteristics list can take any form that is useful to you. If you think you might use it later in a summative report, or as a vehicle for giving formative monitoring reports to staff, consider using a format like the one in Table 3, page 59. This table can serve as a standard against which to measure implementation. For summative evaluation, Table 3 could convey adequacy of implementation by adding two additional columns at the right:

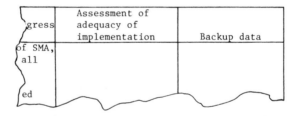

You might prefer to begin with a less elaborate materials/activities/ administrative features list than is shown in Table 3. The following example presents a simpler one.

Example. The proposal for Emerson School's peer tutoring program contained the following paragraph: "... Tutoring activities will take place three days a week in the third, fourth, and fifth grade classrooms during the 45-minute reading period. Group 1 (fast) readers will each be assigned one slower reader whose reading seatwork will become their responsibility. All tutoring will be done using the exercises in the "Read and Say" workbooks which were purchased for the program. During tutoring, one teacher and one aide per classroom will circulate among student pairs, answering questions and informally monitoring the progress of tutees. Tutor-tutee rotation will take place every two months ..."

TABLE 3

Program Ex-Cell Implementation Description

Program Component:
4th Grade Reading Comprehension--Remedial Activities

Person responsible for implementation	Target group	Activity	Materials	Organization for activity	Frequency/duration	Amount of progress expected
Teacher	Students	Vocabulary drill and games	SMA word cards, 3rd & 4th level Teacher-developed word cards, vocabulary Old Maid	Small groups (based on CTBA vocabulary score) Same Same	Daily, 15-20 minutes Same Same	Completion of SMA, Level 4, by all students None specified None specified
Teacher/Aide	Students	Language experience activities --keeping a diary, writing stories	Student notebooks, primary and elite typewriters	Individual	Productions checked weekly (Fridays); students work at self-selected times or at home	Completion of at least one 20-page notebook by each child; 80% of students judged by teacher or aide as "making progress"
Reading specialist/teacher, student tutors	Students	Peer tutoring within class, in readers and workbooks	United States Book Company Urban Children reading series and workbooks	Student tutoring dyads	Monday through Thursday, 20-30 minutes	Completion of 1+ grade levels by 80% of students
Principal	Parents	Outreach--inform parents of program; encourage at-home work in Urban Children texts; hold two Parents' nights; periodic conferences		All parents for program come to Parents' Night; other contact with parents on individual basis	Two Parents' Nights--Nov. and Mar.; 3 written progress reports in Dec., Apr., June; other contact with parents ad hoc	

The assistant principal, given the job of monitoring the program's proper implementation, constructed for her own use a list of program characteristics which included her own informal notes:

```
                    Peer-Tutoring Activities

From written plan
 ˙ Frequency--3 times a week

 ˙ Duration--45-minute session

 ˙ Who--3rd, 4th, 5th graders

 ˙ Where--classrooms

 ˙ Fast readers teach slower

 ˙ Must "have responsibility"--what does this mean?
   (Director says it just means they will tutor same
   child all the time)

 ˙ All tutoring from "Read and Say"--in order, or can
   they skip around?  (Third grade teacher says in
   order)

 ˙ Teacher and aide travel from pair to pair

 ˙ They "monitor"--is there a formal record-keeping
   system?  (Director says yes--recording sheets have
   been drawn up and provided)

 ˙ Tutor-tutee rotate after two months

Additional data from interview with Bill Cox, Reading
Specialist and Project Director, and Ms. Jones, third
grade teacher:
 ˙ 3rd, 4th, and 5th grade tutors in their own class-
   rooms; no switching rooms

 ˙ Teachers and aides--any difference in roles vis-à-
   vis tutors?  No

 ˙ What did average readers do?  Worked alone or in
   pairs with other average readers; tutored when a
   tutor was absent--does this cause disruptiveness?
```

Composing a list of critical characteristics is the first step in each of the data gathering procedures outlined in Chapters 4, 5, and 6.

Creating a Sampling Strategy

Unless the program you are examining is short and simple, *you will not be able to collect and transcribe data on every student and activity over* the course of the entire program. What is more, there is no need to cover the entire spectrum of sites, participants, events, and activities in order to produce a complete and credible evaluation. But you will need to decide *early* where the implementation information you do collect will come from. Specifically you must plan:

- Where to look
- Whom to ask or observe
- When to look—and *how* to sample events and times

Where to look

The first decision concerns *how many* program sites you should examine. Your answer to this will be largely determined by your choice of measurement method; a questionnaire, for instance, can reach many more places than can an observer. Unless the program is taking place in just a few places, close together, it will probably not be practical or necessary to examine implementation at all of them. *A representative sample will provide you with sufficient information to be able to develop an accurate portrayal of the program.*

Solving the problem of *which* sites constitute a representative sample requires that you first group them according to two sets of characteristics:

1. Features of the *sites* that could affect how the program is implemented—such as size of the population served, geographical location, number of years participating in the program, amount of community or administrative support for the program, level of funding, teacher commitment to the program, student or staff traits or abilities

2. Variations permitted in the *program* itself that might make it look different at different locations—such as amount of time given to the program per day or week, choice of curricular materials, or omission of some program components such as a management system or audiovisual materials.[15]

The list of such features is long and unique to each evaluation. For your own use, choose four or so likely sources of major program divergence across sites and classify the sites accordingly. Then, based on how many sites you think you can examine, try to randomly choose some to represent each classification. You can, of course, select some sites for intensive, perhaps even case, study and a pool of others to examine more cursorily.

---

15. Where possible, including a few comparable sites which have not installed the program at all will give you a basis for interpreting some of the data you collect. This will help you determine, for instance, whether the absentee rate in the program is unusual or how much added effort is required from instructors. You can gather similar comparison data by monitoring or asking about usual practice at the program sites before it was initiated.

Whom to ask or observe

Regardless of the size of the program or how many sites your implementation evaluation reaches, you will eventually have to talk with, question, or observe *people.* In most cases, these will be people both *within* the program—the participants whose behavior it directs—and those *outside*—parents, administrators, contributors to its *context.* Answers to questions about whether to *sample* people depend, as with your choice of sites, on the measurement method you will use and your time and resources.

Whom you approach for information also depends on the willingness of people to cooperate, since implementation evaluation nearly always intrudes on the program or consumes some staff time. If you plan to use questionnaires, short interviews, or observations that are either infrequent or of short duration, then you probably can select people randomly. In these cases, having a *person in authority* introduce you and explain your purpose will facilitate cooperation.

If you intend to administer questionnaires or interviews *for other purposes,* perhaps to measure people's attitudes, you may be able to insert a few implementation questions into these. It is often possible, and good practice, to consolidate instruments.

At times your measurement will require a good deal of cooperation. This is the case with requests for record-keeping systems that require continuous maintenance; intensive observation, either systematic or responsive/naturalistic; and questionnaires and interviews given periodically over time to the same people. If data collection requires considerable effort from the staff, and you have too little authority to back your requests, then you should probably ask for voluntary participants. Possible bias from volunteerism can be checked through short questionnaires to a random sample of other staff members. The advantage of gathering information from people willing to cooperate is that you will be able to report a complete picture of the program.

Exactly *which* people should you question or observe? Answers to this will vary, but here are some pointers:

- Ask people, of course, who are likely to know—key staff members and planners. If you think that these people might give you a distorted view, your audience will likely think so too. Thus you should back up what official spokespersons tell you by observing or asking others.

- Some of the *others* should be students if possible. Good information also comes from support staff members, assistants, aides, tutors, student teachers, secretaries, parents. People in these roles see at least part of the program in operation every day—but they are less likely to know what it is supposed to look like *officially.*

If you intend to observe or talk to people several different times over the course of the program, then choice of respondents will be partially dependent on your time frame. Choosing which times and events to measure is discussed in the next section.

When to look

Time will be important to your sampling plan if your answer to any of these questions is *yes*:

- Does the program have phases or units that your implementation study needs to describe separately?
- Do you wish to look at the program periodically in order to monitor whether program implementation is on schedule?
- Do you intend to collect data from any individual site more than once?
- Do you have reason to believe that the program will change over the course of the evaluation?
- If so, do you want to write a profile of the program throughout its whole history that describes how it evolved or changed?

In these situations, you will probably have to sample *data collection dates.* First, divide the time span of the program into crucial *segments,* such as beginning, middle, and end; first week, eighth week, thirteenth week; or Work Units 1, 3, and 6. Then decide if you will request information from the *same* sample of people, at *each* time period or whether you will set up a *different* sample each time.

If and when you sample, be sure to return to the pool the sites or staff members selected to provide data during one particular time segment so that they might be chosen again during a subsequent time segment. People (or sites) should not be eliminated from the pool because they have already provided data. Only when you *sample* from the entire group can you claim that your information is representative of the entire group.

Timing of data collection needs additional adjustment for each measurement method. Questionnaires and interviews that ask about typical practice can be administered at any time during the period sampled. Some instruments, though, will make it necessary to carefully select or sample particular *occasions.* You want your *observations,* for instance, to record typical program events transpiring over the course of a typical program day. The records you collect should not come from a period when atypical factors—such as a bus strike or flu epidemic—are affecting the program or its participants. Sampling of specific occasions—days, weeks, or possibly even hours—will be necessary, as well, if you plan to distribute self-report measures which ask respondents to report about what they did "today" or at a specific time.

Figure 2 demonstrates how selection of sites, people, and times can be combined to produce a sampling plan for data collection. In Figure 2, a district office evaluator has selected *sites, people* (roles), and *times* in order to observe a reading program in session. The sampling method is useful because, in essence, the evaluator wants to "pull" representative *events* randomly from the ongoing life of the program. Her strategy is to construct an implementation description from short visits to each of the four schools taking part in the program.

Figure 2 is an example of an *ex*tensive sampling strategy; the evaluator chose to look *a little* at *a lot* of places. Sampling can be *in*tensive as well—it can look a lot at a few places or people. In such a situation, data from a few *sites,* classrooms, or students can be assumed to mirror that of the whole group. If the set of sites or students is relatively *homogeneous,* that is, alike in most characteristics that will affect how the program is implemented, you can randomly select representatives and collect as much data as possible from them exclusively. If the program will reach heterogeneous sites, classrooms, groups of students, etc., then you should select a representative sample from *each* category addressed by the program—for instance, schools in middle class versus schools in poorer areas; or fifth grades with delinquency-prone versus fifth grades with average students. Then examine data from each of these representatives. The strategy of looking intensively at a few places or people is almost always a good idea whether or not you use extensive sampling as well. These intensive studies could almost be called *case studies,* except that most case study methodologists disavow the need to ensure representativeness.

Planning Data Summary and Analysis

There are two possible purposes for an implementation study. The first and major one is, of course, to *describe* the program and perhaps comment about how well it matches what was intended. A second purpose is to examine *relationships*—between program characteristics and outcomes or among different aspects of the program's implementation. Examining relationships means exploring—usually statistically—the hypothesis on which the program is based. *Do smaller classes achieve more? Are periodic planning meetings related to staff morale?*

This section is intended to help you consolidate the data you collect to meet either of these purposes. It has four parts:

- A description of the use of *data summary sheets* for collecting together item-by-item results from questionnaires, interviews, or observation sheets, pages 67 to 71.
- Directions for reducing a large number of narrative documents, such as diaries, or responses to open-ended questionnaires or interviews into a shorter but representative narrative form, pages 71 and 72.

Howard has
program
in session
from 1-3 p.m.

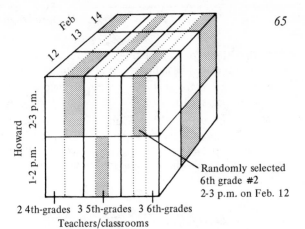

Randomly selected
6th grade #2
2-3 p.m. on Feb. 12

2 4th-grades 3 5th-grades 3 6th-grades
Teachers/classrooms

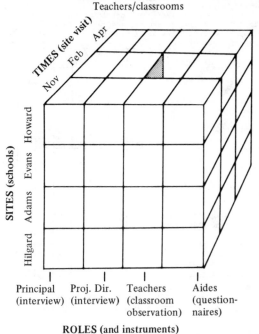

Principal   Proj. Dir.   Teachers   Aides
(interview)   (interview)   (classroom   (question-
                               observation)   naires)

ROLES (and instruments)

Figure 2. Cubes depicting a sampling plan for measuring implementation of a middle-grades reading program in four schools within a district. The large
4x4x3 cube shows the overall data-collection plan
from which sample cells may be drawn. The smaller
cube shows selection of a random sample (shaded
segments) of classrooms and reading periods chosen
at Howard School for observation during a 3-day
February site visit.

- Directions for *categorizing* a large number of narrative documents so that they can be summarized in *quantitative* form, page 73.
- Suggestions for analyzing and reporting quantitative implementation data, pages 74 to 77.

Whether or not you become embroiled in reporting means and percentages and looking for relationships, you will probably have to use the data you collect to underpin a *program description*. Program descriptions are usually presented as narrative accounts or descriptive tables such as Table 3, page 59 or Table 4, below.

TABLE 4

Project Monitoring--Activities[16]

Objective 6: By February 29, 19YY, each participating school will implement, evaluate results, and make revisions in a program for the establishment of a positive climate for learning.

Winona School District
Wiley School

Activities for this objective	19XX				19YY					
	Sep	Oct	Nov	Dec	Jan	Feb	Mar	Apr	May	Jun
6.1 Identify staff to participate		I	C							
6.2 Selected staff members review ideas, goals, and objectives		I	P	P	C					
6.3 Identify student needs	U	I	P	C						
6.4 Identify parent needs	U	I	P	C						
6.5 Identify staff needs	U	I	P	C						
6.6 Evaluate data collected in 6.3 - 6.5						I	U	C		
6.7 Identify and prioritize specific outcome goals and objectives			I	U	P	P	C			
6.8 Identify existing policies, procedures, and laws dealing with positive school climate	U	I	P	P	C					

Evaluator's Periodic Progress Rating:
I = Activity Initiated P = Satisfactory Progress
C = Activity Completed U = Unsatisfactory Progress

Table 4 best suits interim formative reports concerned with how faithfully the program's *actual schedule* of implementation conforms to what was originally planned. A formative evaluator can use this table to report, for instance, the results of monthly site visits to both the program director and the staff at each location. Each brief interim report consists of a table, plus accompanying comments explaining why ratings of "U," unsatisfactory implementation, have been assigned.

---

16. This table has been adapted from a formative monitoring procedure developed by Marvin C. Alkin.

To handle data efficiently, you should prepare a *data summary sheet* for each measurement instrument you use—if possible, at the time you design the instrument. Data summary sheets will help you interpret the backup data you have collected and support your narrative presentation because they assist you in searching for *patterns of responses* that allow you to characterize the program. They also assist you in doing calculations with your data, should you need to do so.

It may seem odd to be concerned about how you will summarize the data at a point where you have barely decided what questions to ask. But it is time-consuming to extract information from a pile of implementation instruments and record, examine, summarize, and interpret it. Thinking about the data summary sheet in advance will encourage you to eliminate unnecessary questions and make sure you are seeking answers at the appropriate level of detail for your needs.

A data summary sheet requires that you have *either closed-response data or data that have been categorized and coded.* Closed-response data include item results from structured observation instruments, interviews, on questionnaires. These instruments produce tallies or numbers. If, on the other hand, you have item results that are narrative in form, as from open-ended questions on a questionnaire, interview, or naturalistic observation report, then you will *first* have to categorize and code these responses if you wish to use a data summary sheet. Suggestions for coding open-response data appear on page 73.

The first part of the following discussion on the use of summary sheets deals with recording and analyzing by hand; the latter part deals with summary sheets for machine scoring and computer analysis.

Preparing a data summary sheet for scoring by hand or by computer

When scoring by hand, you can choose between two ways of summarizing the data: the quick-tally sheet and the people-item roster.

A *quick-tally sheet* displays all response options for each item so that the number of times each option was chosen can be tallied, as in the examples on page 68.

The quick-tally sheet allows you to calculate two descriptive statistics for each *group* whose answers are tallied: (1) *the number or percent of persons who answered each item a certain way,* and (2) *the average response to each item* (with standard deviation) in cases where an average is an appropriate summary. Notice that with a quick-tally sheet, you "lose" the individual person. That is, you no longer have access to individual response patterns. That is perfectly acceptable if all you want to know is how many (or what percentage of the total group) responded in a particular way.

Examples of quick-tally sheets

Questionnaire

```
        uncer-
yes  no  tain
□    □   □      1.   Were the materials available
                     when you needed them?

□    □   □      2.   Were the materials suitable
                     for your students
```

Summary Sheet (quick-tally format)

Item #	yes	no	uncertain
1	ⷭ ︴︴︴︴	︴︴︴	︴︴
2	︴	ⷭ ⷭ ︴︴	︴

etc.

Observation Instrument

```
Rate the quality of the group interaction you
observed using the scale provided.
                1 - unsatisfactory
                2 - poor
                3 - so-so
                4 - good
                5 - outstanding

1 2 3 4 5   1.   The harmony with which the working
                 group functioned

1 2 3 4 5   2.   The involvement of all members in
                 contributing to group planning.
```

Summary Sheet (quick-tally format)

Item #	1 unsatis-factory	2 poor	3 so-so	4 good	5 out-standing
1	︴	︴		︴︴	ⷭ ︴
2		︴︴︴	︴︴︴	ⷭ	

etc.

Often, for data summary reasons or to *calculate correlations,* you will need to know about the response patterns of *individuals* within the group. In these cases, a *people-item data roster* will preserve that information. On a people-item data roster the items are listed across the top of the page. The people (or clàssrooms, program sites, etc.) are listed in a vertical column on the left. They are usually identified by number. Graph paper, or the kind of paper used for computer programming, is useful for constructing these data rosters, even when the data are to be processed by hand rather than by computer. The people-item data roster below shows the results recorded from the filled-in classroom observation response form that precedes it.

Example of a people-item data roster

Observation Response Form (results from classroom 1)

Implementation Objective: Students will direct and monitor their own progress in math activities. During the math period:	applies to most	applies to some	applies to a few	applies to none
1. Students worked on individual math assignments.	4	3 ✓	2	1
2. Students asked for help with finding materials to work on.	1	2	3	4 ✓
3. Students loitered about, working at no activity in particular.	1	2	3	4 ✓
4. Students used self-testing sheets.	4	3 ✓	2	1
5. Students sought out aide ~~...~~ testing				✓

Summary Sheet (people-item format)

	Item 1	Item 2	Item 3	Item 4	Item 5	Item 6	etc.
Classroom 1	3	4	4	3	4	4	
Classroom 2							
Classroom 3							

etc.

The small numerals in the response cells of the observation response form indicate points assigned to each answer for scoring. Unless necessary, they should *not* appear on the response form when it is used by the observer. Since the items in the above example can go in either direction—"applies to none" can be a desirable or undesirable response depending on the item wording—the most desirable response is coded "4" and the least desirable response is coded "1." Besides permitting you to calculate the same descriptive statistics as the quick-tally sheet, the people-item data roster will allow you to compute a total or average score for each person, classroom, etc.

The following example shows a data roster from a classroom observation study in which *three observers* took part. The evaluator has chosen to record the scores in such a way as to keep the observers' responses separate from one another. The major interest, however, remains that of obtaining scores for each of the classrooms. Setting up the summary sheet in this way gives the additional benefit of providing a display for a quick check on interrater reliability, that is, consistency across observers.

Example

Observation Instrument (from observer 1 for classroom 1)

```
Rate the quality of the group interaction you
observed using the scale provided.
            1 - unsatisfactory
            2 - poor
            3 - so-so
            4 - good
            5 - outstanding

1.  The harmony with which the working group func-
    tioned.
            1       2       3      (4)      5

2.  The involvement of all members in contributing
    to group planning.
            1       2      (3)      4       5

3.  The ability of the group to proceed without
    teacher assistance.
            1       2      (3)      4       5
```

Summary Sheet (people-item format)

		Item 1	Item 2	Item 3	etc.
Classroom 1	Observer 1	4	3	3	
	Observer 2				
	Observer 3				
	AVERAGE				
Classroom 2	Observer 1				
	Observer 2				
	Observer 3				
	AVERAGE				

etc.

Mechanical data processing, including computer analysis of data and machine scoring of actual instruments, will either affect the format of the data summary sheet, or make it unnecessary to have one at all. Since computer analysis and machine-scored testing are becoming increasingly accessible to schools and districts, it is possible that you can conserve your own time by investigating these services. Call your district research and evaluation office, or a few local data processing companies. If you find that mechanical data processing fits your time and budget constraints, then your data-summary sheet will need to conform to the machine's requirements. You might even find that your recording form if formatted properly, can be *read and scored* by machine, or that you can use a machine-scorable answer sheet. You can find additional information about computer analysis of your data by referring to the books suggested at the end of the chapter.

How to summarize a large number of written reports into shorter narrative form

If you have to summarize answers to open response questionnaire items, diary or journal entries, unstructured interviews, or narrative *reports* of any sort, you will want a systematic way to do this.

1. Obtain several sheets of plain paper to use as tally sheets. Divide each paper into about four cells by drawing lines.

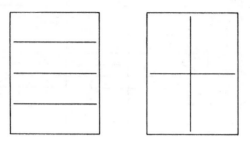

2. Select one of the reports, and look for the kinds of situations or events it describes. As soon as an event is described, write a short summary of it in a cell on one of the tally sheets. In one corner of the cell, tally a "|" to indicate that that statement has been made in one report. As you read the rest of the report, every time you come upon a previously unmentioned event, summarize it in a cell and give it a single tally for having appeared in one report.
3. Read the rest of the reports in any order. Record *new* statements as above. When you come upon one that *seems to have been mentioned in a previous report,* find the cell that summarizes it. Read carefully, making sure that it is more or less the same kind of event. Record another "|" in the cell to show that it has been mentioned in another report. If some *part* of an event or opinion differs substantially from or adds a significant element to the first, write a statement that covers this different aspect in another cell so that you may tally the number of reports in which this new element appears.
4. Prepare summaries of the *most frequent* statements for inclusion in *your* report. There may be good reasons for recording separately data from different groups if the reporters faced circumstances that would predictably bring about different results (e.g., different grade levels, different program variations). Also, if the quantity of the data that you are gleaning from the reports appears to be unwieldy, you may find it necessary to organize the events mentioned into different categories—in some cases more general, in others more narrow. Whenever new summary categories are formed, however, you are cautioned to avoid the blunder of trying to transfer previous tallies from the original categories. The only safe procedure is to return to the original source, the reports themselves, and then tally results for the new categories.

How to summarize a large number of written reports by categorizing

The following procedure helps you to assign numerical values to different types of responses and use this data in further statistical analyses. Suppose, for example, you asked 100 teachers to describe their experiences at a Teacher Learning Center where they received in-service training in class-room management techniques. After reading their reports and summa-rizing them for reporting in paragraph form, you wonder how closely the practices of the Teacher Center conform to the official description of the instruction it offers. You can find this out by *categorizing* teachers' reports into, say, five degrees of closeness to official Teacher Center descriptions—very close, through so-so, to downright contradictory—giving each teacher an opinion score, 1 through 5. Such rank-order data will give you a quantitative summary of teachers' experiences of the program. Perhaps you could then correlate this with their liking for the program or their achievement in courses.

The difficulty of the task of categorizing open-response data will vary from one situation to another. Precise instructions for arriving at your categories and summarizing your data cannot be provided, but the follow-ing advice should help make the task more manageable:

1. Think of a *dimension* along which program implementation might vary—closeness of fit to the program plan, perhaps, or approximation to a theory, or effectiveness of instruction. The dimension you choose should characterize the kinds of reports given to you so that you can put them in order from desirable to undesirable.
2. Read what you consider to be a representative sampling of the data— about 25%. Determine if it is possible to begin with three general categories: (a) clearly desirable, (b) clearly undesirable, and (c) those in between.
3. If the data can be divided in these three piles, you can then put aside for the moment those in categories (a) and (b) and proceed to refine category (c) by dividing it into three piles:

   • Those that are more desirable than undesirable
   • Those that are more undesirable than desirable
   • Those in between

4. Refine categories (a) and (b) as you did (c). If you cannot divide them into three gradations along the dimension you have chosen, then use two; or if the initial breakdown seems as far as you can go, leave it as is.
5. Have one or more people check your categories. This can be done by asking others to go through a similar categorization process or to critique the categories and the selections you have made.

Some suggestions for analyzing and reporting quantitative implementation data

Computing results characteristic by characteristic. If you want to report *quantitative* information from your implementation instruments, this section is designed to help you. It assumes that you have first transferred data to a summary sheet.

Your implementation data depict the frequency, duration, or form of critical characteristics of the program. If you want to explore relationships between certain program characteristics and others, or between program features and achievement or attitude outcomes of the program, then you want to make statements on the nature of: "Programs which had characteristic K tended to J." Here K is a description of the frequency or form of a particular program feature, and J is an achievement, the attitude in a particular group, or perhaps the frequency or form of yet another program feature. You might, for instance, want to see whether programs with more than two aides in the classroom show higher staff morale; or perhaps whether experience-based high school vocational programs with a wide choice of work study plans have fewer dropouts.[17]

Showing this relationship can be done in two ways:

- You can use instrument results (K) to classify programs and then calculate the average J per program, or
- You can *correlate* K with J.

Before you bother to compute a statistic, you should be clear about the question you are trying to answer, and consider who would be interested in the answer and what impact it might have.

If you decide to explore relationships of this sort, you have two choices about what to use for K (and J, if it is another program feature):

1. K can be a summary of responses to a *single item.* It could be, for instance, a classification of schools by funding level of the program, or the average number of participating classrooms at a site. It could be the number of parent volunteers, the number of years the program has been in operation, or observers' estimate of the average amount of time spent at a particular activity. If you use a single item to determine this classification, then make sure that the item gives valid and reliable

---

17. A brief description of an evaluation that related the "degree of implementation" of individualized elementary science programs with school district characteristics such as innovativeness can be found in Evans, W. J., & Sheffler, J. W. Assessment of curriculum implementation. *Planning and Changing,* 1976, *7,* 80-85. The article is a good example of the styles of thought and reporting that characterize implementation studies that seek out relationships.

information. The probability of making an error when answering one item is usually so large that people might be skeptical. If you must use a single item to indicate K, then make sure you can verify what the item tells you. If the classification according to program characteristics which gives you K is critical to the evaluation, you should probably use multiple measures or an *index* to estimate K.

2. You can calculate an *index* to represent K by combining the results of several items or several different implementation measures. A procedure that asks about slightly different aspects of the same characteristic several times, and then combines the results of these questions to indicate the presence, absence, or form of the characteristic, is less likely to be affected by the random error that plagues single questions. An index, therefore, is a more reliable estimate of K than the results of a single item.[18]

If a program plan, or perhaps a theory, has guided your examination of the program, then a particularly useful index for summarizing your findings at each site might be an estimate of *degree of implementation*. How you calculate such an index will vary with the setting. You would, however, select a set of the program's few most critical characteristics, and then compute the index from judgments of how closely the program depicted by the data from one or more instruments has put these into operation. The simplest index of degree of implementation would result from a checklist on which observers note *presence* or *absence* of important program components. The index would equal the number of *present* boxes checked.

Computing results for item by item interpretation. In addition to, or instead of, drawing relationships in your data, you may simply want to report results from your implementation instruments item by item. There are myriad ways to summarize and display this kind of data. Most of these are beyond the scope of this book, and you should consult a book on data analysis and reporting for more detailed suggestions.[19]

---

18. A quick way to compute an index is to add or average the results from several items or instruments. To produce a more credible and, therefore, useful instrument, it is a good idea to item analyze the different questions or instrument results which contribute to the index. The method for doing this is similar to that for constructing an attitude rating scale. Directions for computing indices and developing attitude rating scales can be found in Henerson, M. E., Morris, L. L., & Fitz-Gibbon, C. T. How to measure attitudes. In L. L. Morris (Ed.), *Program evaluation kit.* Beverly Hills: Sage Publications, 1978.

19. See in particular, Fitz-Gibbon, C. T., & Morris, L. L. How to calculate statistics; Morris, L. L., & Fitz-Gibbon, C. T. How to prepare an evaluation report; Henerson, M. E., Morris, L. L., & Fitz-Gibbon, C. T. How to measure attitudes. In L. L. Morris (Ed.), *Program evaluation kit.* Beverly Hills: Sage Publications, 1978.

For the purpose of summarizing responses to individual items, you might want to present totals, percentages, or group averages. In some instances, computation will involve nothing more than adding tallies:

Example. Of the 50 children interviewed, 19 boys and 13 girls reported having taken part in the after-school recreation program. These 32 children reported having engaged in the following activities:

	boys	girls	total
handball	19	7	26
bars and rings	16	12	28
team games (baseball, kickball)	17	10	27
handicrafts	12	12	24
chess	8	8	16
checkers	10	8	18

In other cases, you may want to convert the numbers to percentages:

Example. Observers used a coded behavior record method to record teacher/student question/answer contacts during one week of lab periods in a high school chemistry program. From these extensive coded behavior records, the evaluator was able to find 503 teacher/student question/answer contacts. The evaluator classified these according to the following code:

t—teacher	q—asks a question
s—student	r—gives a response
	o—says nothing

According to this code, tq-sr-tq means that a teacher asked a question, a student gave a response, and the teacher asked another question. Accordingly, different sorts of conversation patterns, plus their relative frequencies, could be broken down as follows:

tq-sr-tq	*tq-sr-tr*	*tq-sr-to*	*sq-tq*	*sq-tr*	*sq-to*	*other*
90 (18%)	45 (9%)	42 (8%)	102 (20%)	80 (16%)	34 (7%)	110 (22%)

It was noted that the frequency of teacher questioning after student response was relatively high. This was a desirable behavior that the program had sought to foster.

If questions on the instrument demand answers that represent a *progression,* you may wish to report an *average answer* to the question.

```
What percent of the period did the teacher spend on disci-
pline?
☐ virtually none            ☐ about 75%
☐ about 25%                 ☐ nearly all the time
☐ close to half
```

Averages can be graphed, displayed, and used in further data analyses. Be careful, however, to assure yourself that the average is truly representative of the responses that you received. If you notice that responses to a particular question pile up at two ends of the continuum, then the answers seem to be *polarized* and averages will not be representative. To report such a result by an average would be misleading to the audience.

For Further Reading

On the topic of sampling . . .

Cochran, W. G. *Sampling techniques.* New York: Wiley, 1953.

Fitz-Gibbon, C. T., & Morris, L. L. How to design a program evaluation (Chapter 8: How to randomize). In L. L. Morris (Ed.), *Program evaluation kit.* Beverly Hills: Sage Publications, 1978.

Sudman, S. *Applied sampling.* New York: Academic Press, 1976.

Weisberg, H. F., & Bowen, B. D. *An introduction to survey research and data analysis.* San Francisco: W. H. Freeman and Co., 1977.

About data summary and analysis . . .

Fitz-Gibbon, C. T., & Morris, L. L. How to calculate statistics. In L. L. Morris (Ed.), *Program evaluation kit.* Beverly Hills: Sage Publications, 1978.

Henerson, M. E., Morris, L. L., & Fitz-Gibbon. How to measure attitudes. In L. L. Morris (Ed.), *Program evaluation kit.* Beverly Hills: Sage Publications, 1978.

Morris, L. L., & Fitz-Gibbon, C. T. How to present an evaluation report. In L. L. Morris (Ed.), *Program evaluation kit.* Beverly Hills: Sage Publications, 1978.

Talmage, H. *Statistics as a tool for educational practitioners.* Berkeley: McCutchan, 1976.

Chapter 4

Methods For Measuring Program Implementation: Records

Records are the tangible remnants of program occurrences. They enable you to reconstruct a credible portrayal of what has gone on in the program. Table 5 lists some commonly kept records. Though any of them could be used to back up your description of a program, you will find the clearest *overall* picture of the program in records that have been kept systematically and regularly.

TABLE 5
Records Often Produced by Educational Programs

- Attendance and enrollment logs
- Progress charts and checklists
- Certificates of completion of activities
- Sign-in and sign-out sheets
- Parental permission slips
- Completed student workbooks
- Logs, journals, and diaries kept by students, teachers, or aides
- Unit or end-of-chapter tests
- Teacher-made tests
- In-house memos
- Newspaper articles, news releases
- Dog-eared and worn textbooks
- Flyers announcing meetings
- Circulation files kept on books or other materials

- Records of bookstore or cafeteria purchases or sales
- Legal documents such as licenses, insurance policies, rental agreements, leases
- Diplomas or transcripts
- Report cards
- Letters of recommendation
- Bills, purchasing orders, and invoices from commercial firms providing goods and services
- Activity or field-trip rosters
- Student assignment sheets
- Products produced by students, such as drawings, lab reports. poems, themes and essays
- Letters to and from parents, business persons, the community

If you want to measure program implementation by means of records, consider two things:

- How can you make good use of *existing* records?
- Can you *set up* a record-keeping system that will give you needed information without burdening the staff?

Where records are already being kept, you can use them as a source of information about the activities they are intended to record. Since the progress charts, attendance records, enrollment forms, and the like kept for the program will seldom cover all you need to know, though, you might try to arrange for the staff or students to maintain additional documents. Of course, you will be able to *set up* record-keeping only if your evaluation begins early enough during program implementation to allow for an accurate picture of what has occurred.

In most cases, it is not realistic to expect that the staff will keep records over the course of the program solely to help *you* gather implementation information, unless these records are easy to maintain (e.g., parent-aide sign-in sheets) or are useful for their own purposes as well. You will do best if you come up with a valid reason why the staff should keep records, and attempt to align your information needs with theirs. You could, for instance, gain access to records by offering a service. One evaluator was able to monitor program implementation at school sites statewide by helping schools write the periodic reports that had to be submitted to the State Department of Education.

Implementation Evaluation Based On Already Existing Records

The following is a suggested procedure to help you find pertinent information within the program's already existing records, and to extract that information.

Step 1. Construct a program characteristics list

Compose a list of the materials, activities and/or administrative procedures about which you need backup data. This procedure was detailed in Chapter 3, pages 57 to 60.

Step 2. Find out from the staff or the program director what records have been kept and which of these are available for your inspection.

Be sure you are given a complete listing of every record that the program produced, whether or not it was kept at every site. Probe and suggest sources that might have been forgotten. Draw up a list of all records that will be available to you.

If part of your task is to show that the program as implemented represents a departure from past or common practice, you might include records kept *before* the program.

Step 3. Match the lists from Steps 1 and 2

For each type of record, try to find a program feature about which the record might give information. Think about whether any particular record might yield evidence of:

- The *duration* or *frequency* of a program activity
- The *form* that the activity took, what it typically looked like; you will find this information only in narrative records such as curriculum manuals and logs, journals, or diaries kept by the participants
- The extent of student or other participant involvement in the activities—attendance, good behavior, etc.

Do not be surprised if you find that few available records will give you the information you need. The program staff has maintained records to fit its own needs; only *sometimes* will these overlap with yours.

Step 4. Prepare a sampling plan for collecting records

General principles for setting up a data collection sampling plan were discussed in Chapter 3, page 60. The methods described there direct you either to sample typical *periods* of program operation at diverse sites, or to look intensively at randomly chosen cases. Were you to use the former method for describing, say, a language arts program, you might ask to see "library sign-in sheets and circulation files for the *fall quarter* at *Baxter Junior High*," as well as for other times and other places, all randomly chosen. The latter method directs that you focus on a few sites in detail. An intensive study might cause you to choose Baxter as representative of participating junior high schools and examine its whole program *in addition to* the library component. You could, as well, find your own way to mix the methods.

If part of your program description task involves showing the extent to which the program is a departure from usual practice, you could include in the sample *sites not receiving the program* and use these for comparison.

Step 5. Set up a data collection roster, and plan how you will transfer the data from the records you examine

The data roster for examining records should look like a questionnaire—

"How many people used the library during this particular time unit?"

"How long did they stay?" "What kinds of books did they check out?"

Responses, entered by your data transfers, can take the form of tallies or answers to multiple choice questions.

When data collection is complete, you might still have to transfer it from the multitude of rosters or questionnaires used in the field, to single data summary sheets, described in Chapter 3, pages 67 to 71.

Step 6. Where you have been able to identify available records pertinent to examining certain program activities, set up a means for obtaining access to those records in such a way that you do not inconvenience the program staff.

Arrange to pick up the records or copy them, extract the data you need, and return them as quickly and with as little fuss as possible. A member of the evaluation staff should fill out the data summary sheet; *program* staff should not be asked to transfer data from records to roster.

Setting Up a Record-Keeping System

The following is a suggested procedure for setting up a record-keeping system. While evaluators seldom have the luxury of building provisions for their own record-keeping into the program itself, be prepared to take advantage of the opportunity when you can.

Step 1. Construct a program characteristics list[20]

Compose a list of the materials, activities, and/or administrative procedures about which you need backup data. This procedure was outlined on pages 57 to 60.

Attach to your list, if possible, columns headed in the manner of Columns 2 and 3, Table 6, page 83. This table has been constructed to accompany an example illustrating the procedure for setting up a record-keeping system.

Example. Ms. Gregory, Director of Evaluation for a mid-sized school district, is intending to evaluate the implementation of a State-funded compensatory education program for grades K through 3. The program uses individualized instruction. After examining the program proposal and discussing the program with various staff members, she has constructed the implementation record-keeping chart shown in Table 6.

---

20. You might need to describe the implementation of more than one program, perhaps because the evaluation uses a control group design, or because one of your tasks is to show that the program represents a departure from usual practice in the school or district. In any case, you will need to repeat this step for each program you describe.

TABLE 6
Example of an Implementation
Record-Keeping Chart

Column 1 Activities (3rd grade)	Column 2 Record to be used for monitoring the activity--adequate for assessing implementation?	Column 3 Frequency and regularity of record collection--sufficiently representative to assess implementation?
1) Early morning warm-up, group exercise (10 min./day)		
2) Individualized reading (45 min./day) Each student: a) reading aloud with teacher/ aide (3 times/week) or b) reading cassette work at recorder center (3 times/ week) or c) reading seatwork--choice of workbook or library book		
3) Perceptual-motor time (15 min./day in school gym with aide) Two parts: a) clapping rhythm exercise (in group) b) open balance period (individual, on jungle gym, balance beam, etc.)		

Step 2. Find out from the program staff and planners which records will be kept during the program as it is currently planned

Be sure this list includes tests to be given to students, reports to parents, assignment cards—all records that will be produced over the course of the program.

Step 3. For each characteristic of your list from Step 1, do the following

First, examine the list of records that will be available to you. Will any of them be useful as a check of either quantity, quality, regularity of occurrence, frequency, or duration of the program characteristic? If it will, enter its name on your activities chart next to the activity whose occurrence it will demonstrate. Jot down a judgment of whether the record *as is* will fit your needs or whether it might need slight modification. Also enter the number of collections or updatings of the record that will take place over the course of the program. If the number of collections seems insufficient to give a good picture of the program, talk to the staff to request more frequent updating.

When you have finished your review of records that will be available, look closely at the set of program activities about which you still need information. These will *not* be covered by the staff's list of planned records. Try to think of ways in which alteration or simple addition to one of the records already scheduled for collection might give you information on the frequency of occurrence or form of one of the activities on your list. If it appears that slight alteration of a record will give you the information you need, note the name of the record and its planned collection frequency and request that the program staff make the change you need.

Example continued. Ms. Gregory found that program teachers *already planned* to keep records of students' progress in "reading aloud" (Activity 2a) and of their work with audio tapes in the "recorder corner" (2b). Further, this record collection *as planned* seemed to Ms. Gregory to give her exactly the implementation information she needed: teachers planned to monitor reading via a checksheet that would let them note the date of each student's reading session and the number of pages read.

Teachers also planned to note the quality of student performance, a bit of data that Ms. Gregory did *not* need. Work with cassettes in the recorder corner (2b) was to be noted on a special form by an aide, but *only* the progress of children with educational handicaps would be recorded. These audio corner records, Ms. Gregory decided, would not be adequate. She needed data on *all* children's use of the tapes. She noted the usefulness of this information on her chart, with an additional notation to speak to the staff about changing record-keeping in the recorder center to include at least a periodic random sample from the whole class.

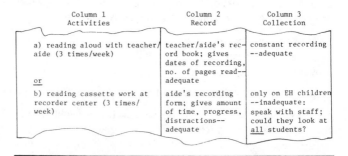

Column 1 Activities	Column 2 Record	Column 3 Collection
a) reading aloud with teacher/aide (3 times/week) or	teacher/aide's record book; gives dates of recording, no. of pages read--adequate	constant recording--adequate
b) reading cassette work at recorder center (3 times/week)	aide's recording form; gives amount of time, progress, distractions--adequate	only on EH children--inadequate: speak with staff; could they look at <u>all</u> students?

If *no* planned record seems as though it will be useful for evaluating the activities that remain, think of one that might be requested from the staff to cover your needs. Before seriously approaching the staff and asking for their assistance with your information collection plan, however, scrutinize it as follows:

- Will it be too time-consuming for the staff to fill out regularly?
- Will the staff members perceive it as useful to *them*?
- Can you arrange a feedback system of any sort to give the staff *useful* information based on the records you plan to ask them to keep?

If the information plan you have conceived passes these checkpoints, suggest it to the staff.

Try to avoid data overload. Do not produce a mass of data for which there is little use. The way to avoid collecting an unnecessary volume of data is to plan data use before data collection.

Example continued. Ms. Gregory needed some information for which no records were planned. For instance, teachers and aides did not intend to keep records of students' participation in "perceptual-motor time" (Activity 3). Ms. Gregory noted this and determined to meet with the staff to suggest some data collection.

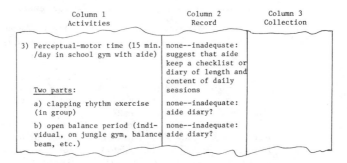

Column 1 Activities	Column 2 Record	Column 3 Collection
3) Perceptual-motor time (15 min. /day in school gym with aide) Two parts:	none--inadequate: suggest that aide keep a checklist or diary of length and content of daily sessions	
a) clapping rhythm exercise (in group)	none--inadequate: aide diary?	
b) open balance period (individual, on jungle gym, balance beam, etc.)	none--inadequate: aide diary?	

Ms. Gregory spoke with aides about the possibility of keeping a diary of perceptual-motor activities. Aides resisted this idea; they wanted the period to be relatively undirected, and they saw it as a break for themselves from regular in-class record-keeping. They did, however, feel that it would be useful to them to have a record of each student's progress in balancing and climbing. Ms. Gregory was thus able to persuade them to construct a checklist called GYM APPARATUS I CAN USE, to be kept by the students themselves and collected once a month. Ms. Gregory decided to collect data on the "clapping" part of the perceptual-motor period in some way other than by examining records, perhaps via a questionnaire to aides at the end of the year, or through observations.

Step 4. Prepare a sampling plan for collecting records

Once you know which records will be kept to facilitate your implementation evaluation, decide where, when, and from whom you will collect them. General principles for setting up a data collection sampling plan were discussed in Chapter 3, page 60. The methods described there produce two types of samples:

- A sample that selects typical time periods or episodes from the program at diverse sites
- A sample that selects people, classes, schools or other sites, considering each *case* typical of the program

Your sampling plan could use either or both.

Example continued. Ms. Gregory was faced with the responsibility of practically single-handedly evaluating a comprehensive year-long program. As it turned out, Ms. Gregory was quite successful at finding records that would provide her with the implementation information she needed. The following records would be made available to her:

- The teachers' record books showing progress in read-aloud sessions
- Aides' recording forms of students' recorder corner work
- Students' GYM APPARATUS I CAN USE checklists

Also available were other records for teaching math, music, and basic science–topic areas not included in the example. All records would be available to Ms. Gregory throughout the year. But how would she find time to extract data from them all?

By means of a time sampling plan, Ms. Gregory could schedule her record collection and data transcription to make the task manageable. First, she chose a *time unit* appropriate for analyzing the types of records she would use. The teachers' records of read-aloud sessions, for example, should be analyzed in *weekly* units rather than daily units. According to Ms. Gregory's activities list, the program did not require students to read every day; they *must* read for the teacher at least three times *per week*. Perceptual-motor time could be analyzed by the day, however, since the program proposal specified a *daily* regimen. She then selected a random sample of *weeks* from the time span of the program and arranged to examine program records at the various sites. She selected *days* for which gym apparatus progress sheets would be examined.

Site and participant selection was random throughout. For each week of data collection, she randomly chose four of the eight participating schools, and within them, two classes per grade whose records would be examined.

Step 5. Set up a data collection roster and plan how you will transfer data from the records you examine

The data roster for examining records should resemble a questionnaire for which answers take the form of tallies or, in some cases, multiple-choice items.

Example continued. Having sampled both time units and classrooms, Ms. Gregory consulted teachers' records from eight classrooms at each grade level for the week of January 26. Once she had prepared a list of the 30 students in one of the third grade samples, she

- Tallied the number of times each one read
- Recorded the number of pages read
- Calculated the mean number of pages read that week per student

Ms. Gregory's data roster for gathering information on third-grade read-aloud sessions from one teacher's record book looked like Table 7.

TABLE 7
Example of a Data Roster
for Transferring Information
From Program Records

Individualized Program

Class: Mr. Roberts--3rd Grade　　School: Allison Park

Activity: Reading aloud with　　Data source: Teach-
teacher or aide　　　　　　　　　er's record book

Questions: How often did children read per week?
　　　　　　How many pages did they cover?

Time Unit: Week of January 26

Student	Tally of times student read		No. of pages read	Mean no. of pages read
Adams, Oliver	////	4	4, 5, 6, 5	5
Ault, Molly	//	2	3, 4	3.5
Caldwell, Maude	///	3	4, 3, 5	4
Connors, Stephen	⧸⧸⧸⧸⧸	5	1, 4, 6, 5, 4	4
Ewell, Leo	///	3	3, 5, 4	4
Goldwell, Nora	⧸⧸⧸⧸⧸	5	6, 2, 3, 4, 5	4
Gross, Joyce	//	2	7, 8	7.5

The data roster is a means for making implementation information accessible to you when you need it so that it can be included in the data analysis for your report. The roster, you will notice, compiles information from a *single* source, covering a single time period. For the purpose of your report, you will usually have to transfer all of the roster data to a *data summary sheet* in order to look at *the program as a whole.* Chapter 3 describes data summary sheets, including those for managing data processing by computer, beginning on page 67.

Step 6. Set up a means for obtaining easy access to the records you need

Gather records from the staff in a way that minimally interferes with their busy work schedules. You, or your delegate, should arrange to collect workbooks, reports, checklists, or whatever, photocopy them or extract the important data, and return these records as quickly as possible. Only in those rare situations where the staff itself is ungrudgingly willing to participate in your data collection should you ask them to bring records to you or transfer information to the roster.

Chapter 5

Methods For Measuring Progam Implementation: Observations

Most audiences consider the observations of people who are not staff members highly credible sources of information about program implementation, and for obvious reasons. Reports of observers are based on what they have *directly seen* while the program was in operation. They have witnessed students talking with teachers and working with program materials; they have explored the classroom or attended planning meetings; they have seen a live enactment of the program. What is more, since they probably have nothing to gain from depicting the program in any particular way, they will not be charged with bias.

Because of the richness and the credibility of the information it can provide, on-site observation is a desirable part of implementation evaluation. Of all implementation measures, observation places the evaluator—or the observers—closest to the operation of the program. Some evaluators feel, in fact, that observation is the only method for capturing and aptly describing a program's complexity.

Setting Up an Observation System: First Considerations

If you intend to gather implementation information using observations, your first task will be to choose a *level of formality*. This decision, like others in evaluation, will depend on your role with regard to the program—whether you are to write a report which summarizes it or to help in its development; your need for credibility; and the relative size of the project. The formality of observation methods forms a continuum from very casual to highly structured, almost ritualized.

Observation at the informal extreme means taking a few quick looks at the program and then preparing a report. This gives you, of course, only general information such as whether the program is taking place *at all* and is free of grave problems. Formal observation demands careful planning, possibly preparation of guidelines for observers to follow, and training of observers. Observation methods at the formal end of the spectrum are concerned with taking a long look at representative parts of the program and recording accurately what was seen.

The credibility demands of most evaluations will probably make it necessary that you conduct more formal observations following a stricter methodology. Informal observation procedures, though appropriate in some situations, are open to challenge by the skeptical audience, who might say:

- *The person observing wasn't prepared, so he didn't know what to look for.*
- *He–or even they–misinterpreted what we were doing.*
- *They came at the wrong time.*

Formal observation methods are careful to prescribe *when* observers watch and how they *record* what they see. They usually provide for training of observers as well as some testing with feedback of sample observation situations. They often make use of disinterested, third party observers—people who have no stake in the implementation evaluation's findings. Clear definition of techniques for gathering implementation information alleviates problems of audience skepticism.

Formal observation methods are of two general types:

- *Systematic* observation in which the observer is told *what to look at beforehand*
- Responsive/naturalistic observation, where the observer arrives on site without a predisposition about what to describe

Responsive/naturalistic observation is not informal, even though it allows the observer to *discover* how to characterize a program. The naturalistic observer, concerned in most cases about capturing the true flavor of the program, constrains when and whom he will observe and follows a discernible method. He spends considerable time observing, taking notes, thinking, and synthesizing. It is not unusual, in fact, for a responsive observer to spend more effort describing a program than an observer who has prepared an instrument in advance.

Making Systematic Observations

The information in this chapter is organized according to the following 12 steps which outline a procedure for designing and using systematic observations:

1. Construct a program characteristics list describing how the program is intended to look.
2. Prepare scenarios of typical program episodes.

3. Prepare scenarios of episodes which should *not* occur.
4. Choose an observation method.
5. Decide how long each observation time sample must be in order to yield good data, and determine how many time samples are needed.
6. Prepare a sampling plan for conducting observations.
7. Prepare the observers' recording sheets.
8. Choose observers.
9. Train observers.
10. Inform the program staff about the forthcoming observations.
11. Conduct observations for the first of the time samples you have chosen from the program's span.
12. When observation data are in, score them and prepare them for interpretation and presentation.

Before you become embroiled in designing your own observation system, look around for one you might adapt—perhaps one that has been used with similar programs before. Pages 112 to 115, for example, describe an observation scheme created at the Stanford Research Institute. It is a good model for observation instruments that record what occurs during class sessions. You might check as well some of the observation instruments you can locate through the sources in For Further Reading, page 116.

The first three steps of the procedure outlined below are intended to help you decide *what to look for*. If you already know what you want to examine, you can begin developing your observation procedure at Step 5. You might, however, want to read over the first four steps to help ensure that you have not overlooked something.

Step 1. Construct a Program Characteristics List

Compose a list of the materials, activities, and/or administrative procedures about which you need backup data. This task, which includes visiting program sites, if possible, to see the program in operation, is outlined on pages 57 to 60.

Step 2. Prepare Scenarios of Typical Program Episodes

Scenarios are short dramatizations of the actions and interactions exhibited by teachers, students, or other participants when the program as planned is in operation. The scenarios augment the list composed in Step 1. That list serves two functions. It gives you an outline of what the program should ideally look like; and it enables you to point to the key materials and arrangements of facilities that should be present, and the activities that should be occurring.

The scenarios build a foundation for designing a systematic observation scheme by helping you to *define* what these program activities might *look like* when they occur. *Where the scenario mentions terms that mean specific actions, these should be defined.* A scenario might stipulate, for instance, that teachers direct *positive or reinforcing comments* to students. You will need to define these terms clearly enough so that observers can agree about which teacher statements are reinforcing or positive and which are not. If the scenario mentions student *play* behaviors, you will have to instruct your observers about what "play" looks like. Should, for example, work with math-related materials *not* assigned by the teacher be classified as play or math instruction? Similarly, you might need to define *attentive* versus *inattentive* behaviors.

Figure 3 shows a scenario for a typical lesson in a phonics-based reading program for first grade. The scenario outlines four aspects of the program:

- The features of the space, in this case the classroom; in another case it could be a play yard, auditorium, or whatever. A scenario might include, as well, a sketch of the layout of the typical place in which observations will occur—if aspects of its arrangement are important to the program.

- Characterization of the materials and other objects relevant to the program which are present. Note that the flashcards in the example are described in terms of *content* and *use.*

- A list of the people involved. The figure notes that the lesson would usually be conducted by the teacher and that an aide is rare.

- Narrative depiction of the activities in which people are taking part. This depiction is both general and specific. The *general* depiction describes the actions of groups of people over a considerable duration of time. For example, reading rotates from child to child until the story is finished. *Specific* activities describe the words or gestures of individuals at a certain time. For example, when a child makes an error reading a word, the teacher initiates the sounding and blending procedure standard to the program.

Step 3. Prepare Scenarios of Episodes Which Should Not Occur

These scenarios will list alternative but undesirable program features. They will describe the most likely ways in which things can go wrong, so that observers can check for their occurrence. The scenario in Figure 4 describes the behaviors that should not occur during the reading instruction lesson described in Figure 3. For example, the teacher should *not* work with fewer than two children; the story should *not* be given a long introduction; the teacher should *not* omit praise for correct answers.

What the Observers Should Find

1. The classroom. Approximately 30 children are working on individual assignments. The teacher and a group of three or four students are seated in a circle in one corner of the room for the phonics lesson.

2. Objects and materials. The teacher has a deck of flashcards and a primer. Each student has a primer only. The flashcards used by the teacher should contain, for review, some previously learned graphemes and some recently taught. The deck should contain one or two new graphemes or clusters that will appear in the story to be read.

3. People. The primer lesson involves a teacher--or rarely an aide--and three or four students. One or two aides supervise students doing seatwork.

4. Activities--general. The teacher starts the lesson by showing the flashcards one at a time, then questions the students individually about the sound made by the vowel, consonant, or cluster showing on the card. Individual children are asked to respond. Correct answers are praised; when a student gives a wrong answer, the teacher asks for volunteers from the group to correct it. After each child has had a chance to respond correctly to about three letters or clusters, the flashcard section ends and the story is begun.

   After a brief introduction from the teacher, individual students are asked to read aloud. Reading errors are treated by the teacher through a prompting procedure in which the child is persuaded to blend the letters in the word. The reading thus rotates from child to child in the group until the story is completed. When the story is over, the teacher calls on various students to summarize the main points in the story. This group lesson lasts about half an hour; each student in the class takes part in this phonics group about three times a week.

   Activities--specific. Wrong answers during the flashcard section of the lesson elicit a response from the teacher: "No, that's not right. Who else would like to try?" or some similar statement. The teacher introduces the story with a single sentence. Such a sentence hints at the theme of the story; for instance, "This is a story about a rabbit with a peculiar habit."

   When a child reading aloud makes an error or stumbles on a word, the teacher initiates the sounding and blending procedure standard to the program. This procedure is more or less as follows: Teacher-- "What's the first syllable? Look at the first letter. What sound does it make?...Look at the second letter," etc. "Now blend them together." If sounding and blending fail to produce the word after about 45 seconds, the teacher asks: "What kind of word do you think belongs in that place in the sentence? An object word or an action word? Can you guess what the word might be?" If this fails also, the teacher tells the child the word and demonstrates for him how its sound matches its graphic representation.

Figure 3. Scenario of a typical lesson: Phonics Bases of Reading Program, First Grade, Primer Level

---

What Observers Should Not See Taking Place

1. The classroom.

2. Objects and materials. Flashcards may not contain more than three new graphemes or clusters (no story in the primer introduces more than two), and the flashcard deck must contain previously learned ones for review and motivation.

3. People. The teacher should not work with fewer than two nor more than five children at one time.

4. Activities--general. The reading of the primer should occur after the flashcard lesson. The flashcard section of the lesson may not conclude until every child has had a chance to make at least two correct responses even if all are with the same letter. The story may not be given a long introduction. This means an introduction of longer than five sentences.

   Activities--specific. Teachers must not ask for the names of letters on the flashcards, only for their sounds. Students who give names should be corrected in the following way: "Yes, but what is its sound?" The teacher should not fail to praise correct answers and must not make prolonged explanatory responses to incorrect answers. Statements such as, "No, Donald, not \e\; the sound is \i\," or "Come on, Nancy, you got that one right last time" are long enough. When readers are having difficulty with a word in the story, the teacher should not suggest that the child look at the picture. Although stick drawings appear in the primer, attention is not to be called to them. When a child is attempting to identify an unknown word, all attention should be called to the printed word and the clues to be gotten from the words in the story.

Figure 4. Scenario of *un*desirable events of Phonics
Bases of Reading Program, First Grade, Primer Level

The three steps which were just described help you to uncover the critical parts of the program which may be buried in the program proposal, or in the theory, philosophy, or model of schooling held important by the program's planners and staff. Once you have completed the scenarios, show the program planners and staff what you have produced and ask for their comments. In particular, you should ask them which parts of the program they consider absolutely critical as opposed to those which it would be nice to have. If your function is formative, the staff can tell you which parts they want to monitor.

Once you are satisfied that you know which features of the program should be the focus of your observations, you need to choose an observation *method*.

Step 4. Choose an Observation Method

There are three types of instruments that may be useful for systematic observation depending on the circumstances of use:

- On-the-spot checklists
- Coded behavior records
- Delayed report instruments

On-the-spot checklists

Checklists can be used for recording the presence, absence, or frequency of a few behaviors *as they occur.* In some circumstances, they can also be used to check on the duration of an activity. They will not, however, help you to record the exact form, quality, or intensity that a particular behavior exhibited.

Two characteristics of checklists make them particularly useful instruments for small scale evaluations, evaluations done under time and financial constraints, or situations in which the evaluator is a newcomer to the field. First, checklists produce a count of the number of times particular events occurred or particular materials or people were observed. These are easy numbers to work with when summarizing and reporting results. Second, training observers to use a checklist is relatively easy. The evaluator needs only to ensure that the observers understand the definitions of the behaviors in question and can carry out the reporting procedure in the setting.

In general, you should consider using a checklist:

- When you can precisely define the material, situation, activity, or event that needs to be detected and count how many times it has occurred
- When critical features of the program consist largely of materials and observables which stay put rather than activities which have a more dynamic nature

You *can* use checklists for observing the occurrence of particular *behaviors,* for instance, how many times the teacher asks a particular sort of question, but you should probably limit the number of behaviors to 10 or fewer. With more than 10 behaviors to look for, observers not only need to detect and classify the behaviors they witness, but they also have to find the proper place to check on the observation recording sheet. This can lead to confusion and inaccuracies. *Frequency tallying* means noting each occurrence of a discrete behavior. Keeping track of the *frequency* of certain questions in a group discussion, for example, would demand making a check on the observer's tally sheet each time the teacher asks

OBSERVATION CHECKLIST

Learning Through Discovery

Make a check in the proper box each time you see the following behaviors occur during the lesson. Use one sheet for
each lesson observed. For each lesson, record the actions
of the teacher and ONE STUDENT, chosen at random.

Observer _Hellendale_   Class observed _1-C_
Date and time _Nov. 20, 10 am - 10:35_
Curriculum lesson number _29_   Topic _classifying time_
Number of students in lesson group _6_

Teacher tells the students to list the information they
have gathered so far.
    ~~////~~

Teacher asks for a prediction of the results of an action (s)he is about to undertake.
    //

Teacher gives class the answer to a question (s)he has
asked.
    ///

Teacher responds to student comment by "elaborating"
on the student's answer.
    ~~////~~ //

Student writes down a comment made by the teacher, him/
herself, or another student.
    ~~////~~ ~~////~~ ~~////~~ /

Figure 5. An on-the-spot checklist

that kind of question. But activities of some duration such as student seatwork, recess, certain social interchanges, or art period, need to be recorded differently. Measuring *duration* demands that you *time interval sample,* that is, pace observations to the passing of short time intervals, say a few minutes. To track the duration of a group discussion, the observer would record a tally, say one minute, at the end of each predetermined time interval to show that the discussion was *still underway.*

Example of a checklist used for monitoring activity duration. A computer-assisted instruction (CAI) program for teaching fourth-grade spelling is systematically observed for level of student participation. For two weeks an observer watches pupils working at five terminals during the daily 35-minute CAI period. The observer notes the duration of the time that each pupil actually works with the computer spelling program.

Observer __KLEIN__	Time begun __10:40 a.m.__
Date __MAY 10__	Time ended _____
Class __5-D__	Number of 20-second intervals recorded _____

Time Intervals (20 seconds)

Student	Terminal	1 Y	1 N	2 Y	2 N	3 Y	3 N	4 Y	4 N	5 Y	5 N	6 Y	6 N	7 Y	7 N	etc.
SCHWARTZ	A	✓		✓		✓		✓								
SMITH	B	✓			✓											
GARCIA	C	✓		✓		✓		✓								
WONG	D			✓		✓		✓								
O'HARA	E	✓		✓		✓			✓							
JOHNSON	B						✓	✓								
etc.																

Figure 6. Observation checklist for recording duration of time students spend at CAI terminal

Armed with a stopwatch and the checklist in Figure 6, the observer checks each pupil's behavior at the passing of 20-second intervals. If the pupil is working on the program, a check is made in the *yes* column for that interval; if the pupil is looking away or typing but not in response to program requests, then a check is made in the *no* column. The observer also notes whether a student has left the terminal altogether, placing a solid horizontal line in the remainder of that student's row. Then new students who use the terminal are entered at the bottom of the list, and the recording of on-task behavior begins again.

Figure 6 shows recording from one observer of four time intervals for six CAI students. Note that student Johnson replaced student Smith at Terminal B at the beginning of the third 20-second interval.

**Example of use of an observation checklist for tallying the frequency of
behaviors.** The formative evaluator of the phonics program described
earlier in the scenarios wishes to know whether the teachers are implementing correctly the prescribed small group lessons. The sample checklist in Figure 7 was constructed and used by observers watching randomly selected reading lessons.

```
┌─────────────────────────────────────────────────────────────┐
│                   Observation Checklist:                     │
│                   Phonics Bases of Reading                   │
│                                                              │
│  First Grade--Primer Level--Small Group Lesson               │
│                                                              │
│  Observer_____    Class_____     │
│                                                              │
│  Date_____    Time:  From_____to_____       │
│                                                              │
│  On the line next to each behavior, make a check each        │
│  time you see the behavior occur during the lesson.          │
│  You should use one of these lists for every lesson          │
│  observed.                                                   │
│                                                              │
│  Teacher presenting a phonics flashcard                      │
│  asks for the sound of a letter              _____    │
│                                                              │
│  Teacher asks for the name of a letter                       │
│  on the flashcard                            _____    │
│                                                              │
│  Teacher praises a correct answer            _____    │
│                                                              │
│  Teacher introduces a story (make one                        │
│  check per sentence spoken)                  _____    │
│                                                              │
│  Teacher tells a pupil or the group to                       │
│  "look at the picture"                       _____    │
│                                                              │
│  Did the lesson follow the prescribed         ☐        ☐     │
│  sequence?                                   yes       no    │
└─────────────────────────────────────────────────────────────┘
```

Figure 7. Observation checklist for recording
occurrence and frequency of teacher behaviors

Suggestions for assuring good on-the-spot checklists

1. Keep the item number down, preferably below 10.
2. Place the items in logical sequence, perhaps according to the times at which activities occur or the placement of materials or activity areas in the room.
3. Make sure that observers understand your definitions of terms.
4. Decide whether to record just occurrences, or frequencies as well. If you want to know if the behavior occurred at all, single checks will be sufficient.

```
Which math materials were used?
☐ math place-value games
☐ number bingo
☐ number practice cassette tapes
```

If you want to know how frequently an event was observed, you will ask the observers to *tally*.

```
Make a check each time you see one of the following mate-
rials being used:
_____ math place-value games
_____ number bingo
_____ number practice cassette tapes
```

In situations where you want to record the duration of activities, you may want to tally on a time interval sampling basis.

Coded behavior records

Coded behavior records enable you to record in detail many behaviors as they occur within a given time period, but they are the most difficult observation method to use well.

The technique permits you to record not only *what* events occurred *and how many times,* but also to record the *sequence* in which they took place. Assignment of symbols—or codes—to behaviors being observed is essential to coded behavior records. The code system is then taught to observers.

NEW OPPORTUNITIES SCHOOL

Self-Exploration Program
Observation Recording
Sheet

Observer _Mansfield_   Group observed _EH 103_
Date _5·8_   Time of observation: (am) pm

Observation #1

Starting time _11:22_   Ending time _11:37_

TP+	ST-	TP+	TTS	ST-	TTS	TP+	TTS	ST-	TTS
TSS	ST*	TP+	TP+	ST*	TSS	ST+	TE	TTS	TM
TTS	TP+	TE	ST+	TE	TTS	TM	ST+		

Figure 8. A coded behavior record

Here is an example of a relatively simple code system.

Basic Code:

A—teacher	r—requests	p—praises
B—helper	a—assigns	h—helps
C—child being helped	v—volunteers	

Combination of Symbols:

Arv—teacher requests volunteers

AaBC—teacher assigns one child to help another

ApB—teacher praises helper

ApC—teacher praises child being helped

BpC—helper praises child she is helping

Bv—child volunteers to help another child

Bh—child engages in helping behaviors

BrA—helper requests help from teacher

Cr—child requests help

Coded behavior records have two disadvantages that make them difficult data collection methods for most evaluations. First, data from coded behavior records are hard to summarize and interpret. The coded behavior record produces a string of symbols; once the observations have taken place you must still extract data from the records. This usually entails identifying event sequences of interest and then examining the records to tally the occurrence of these sequences. Second, use of the coded behavior record requires that observers be thoroughly trained so that several observers watching the same episode could produce almost the same coded record. This means not only noticing when a target event occurs but also noting its duration and observing accurately the sequence of events in which it is embedded.

Coded behavior records nonetheless are useful under the following circumstances:

- When you want to record the sequence in which events occurred, including sequences perhaps not prescribed

- When you want to get down on paper as much as possible of what the observer sees
- When you must record many different events on the part of teachers, pupils, etc.
- When the amount of time available and your own expertise make it feasible to devise the code for recording behaviors and for training observers
- When you can audio or videotape the events to be recorded so that the observer can check and recheck his codings

Coded behavior records enable you to record many different events because of the flexibility of a code system. The basic code should comprise as few symbols as possible to ensure that observers will neither forget nor confuse them.

Example of a coded behavior record to find out how a program is evolving. An evaluator has been assigned the job of describing and evaluating a group inquiry science program in which teachers hold discussions to help students reason out hypotheses about various physical phenomena. The major directive to teachers, who have been extensively trained in methods of questioning, is to ask questions and make statements so as to prolong verbal interchanges with and among students. The program plan, therefore, specifies no particular type or length of interchange, only that teachers try as hard as possible to make these discussions lengthy. The teachers themselves have described their group discussion strategy in slightly more specific detail. They try to ask only questions that encourage students to use concepts, analysis, and evaluation. They do not ask "yes, no, or right answer" questions, and they try not to disagree outright with the student. Only students who have raised their hands are called on. Teachers try not to give their own opinions on the issues under discussion. They ignore disruptions. In all circumstances they try to keep the discussion going.

To see how well their description fits usual program practice, the evaluator has selected and trained two observers to watch randomly-sampled class discussions. The observers will keep a coded behavior record of each discussion. They will memorize and use a symbol system, excerpts of which comprise Figure 9. The two observers will keep a running account of comments and interactions during randomly selected 20-minute sessions over a two month period. From the strings of interactions recorded, the evaluator will be able to characterize the kinds of verbal interchanges that the program produces. She will be able to tell how many and what type of comments are made as well as what sorts of teacher remarks seem to facilitate or terminate discussion.

```
          Code for Recording Observations
                of Group Discussion

Symbol                        Behavior

  TY      Teacher asks a why question

  TOO     Teacher asks a who question

  TH      Teacher asks a how question

  TD      Teacher makes a disagreeing comment

  TP      Teacher paraphrases a student's comment

  TR      Teacher reprimands a student

  TT      Teacher asks a question or makes a state-
          ment that terminates the exchange

  SO      Student expresses opinion
```

Figure 9. Excerpt from a code for producing a record of science group discussion behaviors

Suggestions for effective use of coded behavior records

1. Devise a *manageable code,* one the observer can easily learn. This means that the number of symbols must be restricted; but combinations of symbols, where possible, can increase the repertoire of possible behavior descriptions.
2. Modify the instrument as your needs require. For example, if you find that the people being observed are likely to engage in the same behavior for a period of time, you may want to build into the instrument a means for distinguishing between behaviors of long and short duration.
3. Design the recording sheets with an eye toward information decoding and interpretation. If the job of transferring coded information to a summary sheet can be done by a clerk or an aide, you will save time. Early attention to precisely how information will be analyzed and reported will prevent collecting unnecessary or uninterpretable data.

Delayed report instruments

Delayed reports of one kind or another are commonly used observation tools. One characteristic that distinguishes them from the two previously discussed techniques is that they are filled in *after* an observation period

Figure 10. A delayed-report observation instrument using time interval sampling

has passed. While the amount of subjective interpretation required of the observer will vary, most delayed report instruments do require some inference or judgment. Delayed report instruments are essentially *questionnaires* which ask about what the observer has seen. In addition to the development of the questionnaire, the delayed report method requires two basic procedures:

1. Observers must be *pre-informed* about what they are looking for. They learn beforehand the nature of the questions on the questionnaire.
2. The observation session should be as formalized as possible. The evaluator decides when it will occur, how long it will last, and who will be observed.

The simplest way to use a delayed report instrument is to have observers watch the program in operation for a specified period of time and then withdraw to fill out the questionnaire. A more complex method, but one which has advantages when you want to watch intensively particular events or people, is to sample time intervals.

Time interval sampling, depicted in Figure 10, is accomplished by dividing the total observation period into short intervals—minutes, or perhaps only seconds long. The observer spends the initial portion of each interval observing and the latter part recording, then switches his attention back to observing and recording again. If *different* individuals or episodes are to be watched, the observer can shift the objects of observation after each time interval.

The delayed report method will be most useful:

- When you feel you can get better data by sampling from the scene periodically rather than recording whole episodes; for example, when you need data on many students working independently.
- When behaviors must be watched so carefully that recording would interfere. The delayed report method allows the observer to devote full attention to what is being seen.
- When there is a possibility that recording would intimidate, fascinate, or otherwise disturb the people being observed. The observer can record outside of the room.

The amount of training needed by observers using a delayed report method varies according to the complexity of the observed events and the amount of judgment you expect the observers to make about what they have seen.

Example of the delayed report method. The evaluator of the phonics program described earlier in the scenarios wishes to describe the silent reading acitivities of students who are *not* taking part in group reading with the teacher. The program plan specifies that students who are working in their seats either (a) use workbooks, or (b) practice drill exercises with audio machines which present flashcards and read words for students. These activities are supervised by classroom volunteers and aides.

The evaluator hires two observers to watch the students' seatwork. Over the course of two weeks, these two observers each watch five students per day during the 20-minute seatwork period. The observers' 20-minutes are divided as follows: They each watch five students for four minutes apiece. Each four minute time interval involves a 3½ minute observation of one student followed by 30 seconds of recording. They then turn their attention to another student, observe for 3½ minutes, and record again.

Suggestions for effective use of delayed report instruments

1. When you write items, check the wording to see if you can reduce the level of observer inference or judgment and still obtain the information you need. Again, by eliminating words likely to be interpreted differently by different observers, you increase accuracy.

2. When you determine the length of observation time units, keep in mind that the longer the delay between observation and recording, the less dependable the rating. You can narrow the time gap by time interval sampling. In this case, be sure to format your recording sheet to reflect division of the observation period into intervals.

3. Before you design the final draft of the instrument, plan how you will analyze and report the results of the observation.

Once you have decided whether to use a checklist, coded behavior record, or a delayed report instrument, you should make a final determination of what behaviors or events you intend to observe. Define them as precisely as possible, and rough out the instrument.

Step 5. Decide How Long Each Observation Time Sample Will Need To Last In Order To Yield Good Data

In systematic observation, any one observer is responsible for watching one or more program participants or episodes for a specified period of time. The length of this time period will vary. In general, of course, time samples should be long enough so that events of interest can be seen. If the events to be recorded by observers go on continuously, then the length of time spent on observation can be as short as a few minutes, and time interval sampling can be used. In this case time interval sampling will give observers a chance to watch many different participants. The length of observation sessions will be further influenced by the *number of observations needed.* Ask yourself:

- How many observations will provide convincing evidence that the findings represent recurring behavior?
- At what point during the overall life of the program should these observations take place?
- What is the best time for the observation: mid-morning? afternoon? early in the week? Fridays? Check with the program staff to find out how they schedule their daily and weekly activities. Find out when the program can be seen.

Step 6. Prepare a Sampling Plan for Conducting Observations

Guidelines for setting up a data collection sampling plan were discussed in Chapter 3, page 60. In that chapter it was suggested that you either draw a sample of typical time periods of program operation at *diverse* sites or choose particular sites or cases for intensive study.

Besides choosing sites and times at which to conduct observations, you will probably need to sample people and events to watch *during* the observation as well. While observing in a classroom, for instance, it will not be possible to watch each pupil and every event. You will have to be selective. If the program prescribes a group activity, then the observer simply watches the group. However, where many individuals or several groups are participating, the decision about whom and what to observe in order to get a fair representation of program events is more difficult.

To help you decide who should be the focus of observation, ask yourself these questions:

- Do you need to focus on the teacher or leader? That is, does the program require specific behaviors from this person?
- Do you need to select some participants from the group because they are to be treated differently or are likely to respond to the program differently? Or are there some people whom you or the evaluation audience believe might have more difficulty than others participating in the program?
- Are you going to *pre-select* the subjects for observation and provide the observers with the names of specific people to watch, or are you going to ask the observer to make on-the-spot selections based on who is nearby or who is engaging in a particular activity?

- Will the observer stay with one participant or group for an entire observation period, or will the subjects of observations change during that period?
- Do you want the observer to make a quick check at any time of what *all* participants are doing?

Under any circumstances, of course, you should try to observe as many participants as possible and have the observers spend as much time at as many program sites as possible. The more of this kind of data you collect, the more representative will be the picture of the program you provide. What and how much you observe will be determined by such practical considerations as the number of observers you can recruit, the number of time samples of the desired length you can fit in every day, and the tolerance of the program staff for having the observers present.

Step 7. Prepare the Observers' Recording Sheets

While the examples of observation methods in Step 4 can help provide a basic format for these methods, you will probably need to adapt the format to your situation.

If your observers are not experienced and know little about the subject which the program addresses, then you will have to train them so that they agree about what they see and can use the observation instrument uniformly.[21] You will also probably have to revise whatever instrument you develop initially—perhaps several times—to eliminate or adjust items with which observers have problems. To help diminish the time investment needed for assuring the fit between observers and instrument, *keep the instrument simple.* A good rule of thumb is to design the instrument so that observers focus on *behaviors* and *events* rather than expressing opinions about these events. The *language* of the items can help with this. For example, a checklist entry could be phrased

```
Student works on math five minutes without looking
away or leaving seat
```

rather than

```
Student is deeply engrossed in math work
```

---

21. In other words, your observation scheme—instrument and observers—should show inter-rater reliability. See Step 9 and pages 135 to 138.

A coded behavior symbol could consist of

    Sr--student raises hand

rather than

    Sn--student knows answer

Similarly, a questionnaire item from a delayed report instrument could ask

    Approximately how many students signed into the math
    resource area during the observation period?
    _____ 0-2   _____ 3-5   _____ 6-8   _____ 9-11

rather than

    How interested did students appear to be in the math
    resource area?

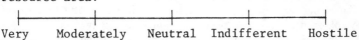

    Very   Moderately   Neutral   Indifferent   Hostile

When looking at some program characteristics, of course, you may *want* observers to make inferences beyond what they see. Some complex events cannot be captured simply by counting the frequency of a particular behavior or event. Such is the case with the two items below, both of which have high inference:

    How would you rate the noise level in the classroom?
    _____ High--adults could not be heard
    _____ Fairly high
    _____ Moderate
    _____ Fairly quiet
    _____ Extremely quiet

What percent of the observation interval would you say the students spent attending to the task at hand?

_____ 80-100%   _____ 20-39%

_____ 60- 79%   _____ less than 20%

_____ 40- 59%

In general, the more inference you allow observers, the richer the portrait you will receive of the program; but you will have to invest much time and effort in amplifying and defining the items and training observers so that their inferences will reflect a common viewpoint.

Step 8. Choose Observers

In the interest of reliability and credibility, try to use at least two observers. If you need to make a strong case for objectivity, the observers should be detached from the program and should stand neither to profit nor suffer as a result of the evaluation. Observers can generally be recruited on a volunteer or minimum salary basis from high schools or local colleges, from other schools in the district, and in the case of a fairly large school, from other departments.

In the case of less formal implementation evaluations you may be able to relax the rules about observer objectivity. In some cases, for example, in an exclusively formative evaluation, it might be useful to have people who planned the program or who are implementing it at another site serve as classroom observers. They may see things that the detached observer would not see or even expect to look for. Their participation as observers may push them to take a good hard look at the program or the progress it is making toward achieving its intended goals.

Step 9. Train Observers and Try Out the Instrument

Explain to your observers what you mean by systematic observation and describe the behaviors they will be watching; train observers in the definitions you will be using to describe the behaviors, materials, and events which should be taking place. If you are using a coded behavior record, train observers to use the code. Make flashcards and hold drills if you have to, and *test* observers for mastery of the definitions and code. Distribute copies of your instrument and explain how to use it. If it will not bias the results of the observation, explain to the observers why you need the information and how it will be used.

Have the observers practice. If you intend to use time interval sampling in which the observer must rapidly rotate between observing and recording, give observers stopwatches or timers and have them practice observing and recording quickly. Role-playing, watching video-tapes, and practice observations in non-program classrooms are all techniques for preparing observers. Have the observers monitor each other and suggest changes in the category codings or behavior classifications if they find your instructions unclear. If necessary, make changes or deletions.

Step 10. Inform the Program Staff About the Forthcoming Observations

To let the staff know about what you intend to do, you can approach people individually, conduct a group meeting, or circulate a memo through the office of the project director or the chief administrator. *Be sure to show in some way that the person in authority sanctions the observations.*

You might want to introduce the observers to the program staff before they observe. No matter how you choose to introduce the observation, explain why the observers will be present and how long they will stay in one room. It is probably not a good idea to tell the staff the exact day or time when the observers will appear. Not knowing when to expect observers will discourage staff from preparing something for the observer that is not typical of the program.

Step 11. Conduct Observations

Make sure the observers carry out the observations as planned. Keep careful track of problems and inconsistencies between raters so that all errors, discrepancies, or unexpected problems can be corrected before the next round of observations or can be reported in the implementation section of the report.

Step 12. When the Observation Data Are In, Score Them, and Prepare Them for Interpretation and Presentation

If your observation system has used either a checklist or questionnaire for recording, you will have to transfer these data from individual instruments to a data summary sheet, described on pages 67 to 71.

If you have used a *coded behavior record,* then you need to further reduce the data by tallying the occurrence of symbols and symbol sequences that are of interest to you. This can be done as follows:

1. Look over the coded sheets and decide which symbols and which symbol sequences you want to report. This may require some careful thought and extensive examination of patterns in the data. Always keep in mind what it is you expect to describe in the report.
2. Construct a tally sheet and tally the number of occurrences of each symbol or sequence per observation or time interval.

3. Calculate the mean number of occurrences of each symbol per group or observation that are of interest to you; for example, those from the same class or taken at the same time over the span of the program. You might also graph the distribution of the symbols, explaining the number of times each occurred per time period observed.

An Observation System You Might Adapt to Your Own Purposes: The Stallings Observation System

A method of measuring program implementation through observation has recently been developed as part of an evaluation of the Federal Follow-Through Program. Authored by Jane Stallings and David Kaskowitz of Stanford Research Institute (SRI), the observation instrument is available for measuring implementation of classroom programs.[22]

Stallings describes the rationale for developing the system in the following way:

> Observation was the only way to see whether or not the Follow-Through Programs were successful in getting their ideas into the classroom. We (the SRI staff) had to see if the materials specified in each program were being used; if children were grouped with classroom aides and teachers as specified; and if the verbal interactions of teachers and children were those specified by the sponsors of the models. (p. 25)

To meet these needs the SRI researchers developed an observation system containing three instruments:

- *A physical environment information form.* With this, the observer describes equipment and material.
- *The classroom observation procedure.* With this, the observer describes the general type of activities occurring in the classroom, coding for each time sample the activities of all students and adults in the room.
- *The 5-minute interaction.* With this, the observer records the specific behaviors comprising interactions among various program participants during a 5-minute observation period.

The first instrument, the physical environment information form, is a checklist. The second instrument, the classroom observation procedure

22. The observation system as first developed is described in Stallings, J. A., & Kaskowitz, D. *Follow-through classroom observation 1972-1973.* Menlo Park, CA: Stanford Research Institute, 1974. The system that is more broadly available, complete with suggestions of its modification for use in various classrooms, is contained in Stallings, J. A. *Learning to look: A handbook on classroom observation and teaching models.* Belmont, CA: Wadsworth Publishing Co., 1977.

reproduced in Figure 11, is also a checklist, but a sophisticated one on which the observer notes, per time sample, the activities of each individual, dyad of two children, small group, and large group in the room.

  CLASSROOM OBSERVATION PROCEDURE

CLASSROOM CHECK LIST (be sure to code EVERYONE in the class)		ONE CHILD	TWO CHILDREN	SMALL GROUPS	LARGE GROUPS
1. Snack, lunch		T ①②③ / A ①②③ / v ①②③ / i ①②③	T ①②③ / A ①②③ / v ①②③ / i ①②③	T ①②③④ / A ①②③④ / v ①②③④ / i ①②③④	T ①② / A ①② / v ①② / i ①②
2. Group time		T ①②③ / A ①②③ / v ①②③ / i ①②③	T ①②③ / A ①②③ / v ①②③ / i ①②③	T ①②③④ / A ①②③④ / v ①②③④ / i ①②③④	T ①② / A ①② / v ①② / i ①②
3. Music	Story, Dancing	T ①②③ / A ①②③ / v ①②③ / i ①②③	T ①②③ / A ①②③ / v ①②③ / i ①②③	T ①②③④ / A ①②③④ / v ①②③④ / i ①②③④	T ①② / A ①② / v ①② / i ①②
4. Arts, Crafts		T ①②③ / A ①②③ / v ①②③ / i ①②③	T ①②③ / A ①②③ / v ①②③ / i ①②③	T ①②③④ / A ①②③④ / v ①②③④ / i ①②③④	T ①② / A ①② / v ①② / i ①②
5. Table Games	Guessing Games, Puzzles	T ①②③ / A ①②③ / v ①②③ / i ①②③	T ①②③ / A ①②③ / v ①②③ / i ①②③	T ①②③④ / A ①②③④ / v ①②③④ / i ①②③④	T ①② / A ①② / v ①② / i ①②
6. Math	Numbers, Arithmetic	T ①②③ / A ①②③ / v ①②③ / i ①②③	T ①②③ / A ①②③ / v ①②③ / i ●②③	T ①●②③④ / A ①●②③④ / v ①②③④ / i ①②③④	T ①② / A ①② / v ①② / i ①②
7. Reading, Alphabet, Lang Development		T ①②③ / A ①②③ / v ①②③ / i ①②③	T ①②③ / A ①②③ / v ①②③ / i ①②③	T ①②③④ / A ①②③④ / v ①②③④ / i ①②③④	T ①② / A ①② / v ①② / i ①②
8. Social Studies, Geography		T ①②③ / A ①②③ / v ①②③ / i ①②③	T ①②③ / A ①②③ / v ①②③ / i ①②③	T ①②③④ / A ①②③④ / v ①②③④ / i ①②③④	T ①② / A ①② / v ①② / i ①②
9. Science, Natural World		T ①②③ / A ①②③ / v ①②③ / i ①②③	T ①②③ / A ①②③ / v ①②③ / i ①②③	T ①②③④ / A ①②③④ / v ①②③④ / i ①②③④	T ①② / A ①② / v ①② / i ①②
10.	Sewing, Cooking, Pounding, Sawing	T ①②③ / A ①②③ / v ①②③ / i ①②③	T ①②③ / A ①②③ / v ①②③ / i ①②③	T ①②③④ / A ①②③④ / v ①②③④ / i ①②③④	T ①② / A ①② / v ①② / i ①②
11.	Blocks, Trucks	T ①②③ / A ①②③ / v ①②③ / i ①②③	T ①②③ / A ①②③ / v ①②③ / i ①②③	T ①②③④ / A ①②③④ / v ①②③④ / i ①②③④	T ①② / A ①② / v ①② / i ①②
12.	Dramatic Play, Dress-Up	T ①②③ / A ①②③ / v ①②③ / i ①②③	T ①②③ / A ①②③ / v ①②③ / i ①②③	T ①②③④ / A ①②③④ / v ①②③④ / i ①②③④	T ①② / A ①② / v ①② / i ①②
13. Active Play		T ①②③ / A ①②③ / v ①②③ / i ①②③	T ①②③ / A ①②③ / v ①②③ / i ①②③	T ①②③④ / A ①②③④ / v ①②③④ / i ①②③④	T ①② / A ①② / v ①② / i ①②
14. RELIABILITY SHEET ○					

Legend at left (applies to items 6–9):
○ TV
○ Audio-Visual Materials
○ Exploratory Materials
○ Math and Science Equipment
● Texts, Workbooks
● Puzzles, Games

Figure 11.   Classroom observation procedure

		ONE CHILD	TWO CHILDREN	SMALL GROUPS	LARGE GROUPS
15. Practical Skills Acquisition		T ① ② ③ / A ① ② ③ / V ① ② ③ / i ① ② ③	T ① ② ③ / A ① ② ③ / V ① ② ③ / i ① ② ③	T ① ② ③ ④ / A ① ② ③ ④ / V ① ② ③ ④ / i ① ② ③ ④	T ① ② / A ① ② / V ① ② / i ① ②
16. Observing		T ① ② ③ / A ① ② ③ / V ① ② ③ / i ① ② ③	T ① ② ③ / A ① ② ③ / V ① ② ③ / i ① ② ③	T ① ② ③ ④ / A ① ② ③ ④ / V ① ② ③ ④ / i ① ② ③ ④	T ① ② / A ① ② / V ① ② / i ① ②
17. Social Interaction Ob [☺ ② ☹]	ⓉⒶⓋ	T ① ② ③ / A ① ② ③ / V ① ② ③ / i ① ② ③	T ① ② ③ / A ① ② ③ / V ① ② ③ / i ① ② ③	T ① ② ③ ④ / A ① ② ③ ④ / V ① ② ③ ④ / i ① ② ③ ④	T ① ② / A ① ② / V ① ② / i ① ②
18. Unoccupied Child		T ① ② ③ / A ① ② ③ / V ① ② ③ / i ① ② ③	T ① ② ③ / A ① ② ③ / V ① ② ③ / i ① ② ③	T ① ② ③ ④ / A ① ② ③ ④ / V ① ② ③ ④ / i ① ② ③ ④	T ① ② / A ① ② / V ① ② / i ① ②
19. Discipline		T ① ② ③ / A ① ② ③ / V ① ② ③ / i ① ② ③	T ① ② ③ / A ① ② ③ / V ① ② ③ / i ① ② ③	T ① ② ③ ④ / A ① ② ③ ④ / V ① ② ③ ④ / i ① ② ③ ④	T ① ② / A ① ② / V ① ② / i ① ②
20. Transitional Activities	ⓉⒶⓋ	T ① ② ③ / A ① ② ③ / V ① ② ③ / i ① ② ③	T ① ② ③ / A ① ② ③ / V ① ② ③ / i ① ② ③	T ① ② ③ ④ / A ① ② ③ ④ / V ① ② ③ ④ / i ① ② ③ ④	T ① ② / A ① ② / V ① ② / i ① ②
21. Classroom Management	ⓉⒶⓋ	T ① ② ③ / A ① ② ③ / V ① ② ③ / i ① ② ③	T ① ② ③ / A ① ② ③ / V ① ② ③ / i ① ② ③	T ① ② ③ ④ / A ① ② ③ ④ / V ① ② ③ ④ / i ① ② ③ ④	T ① ② / A ① ② / V ① ② / i ① ②
22. Out of Room	ⓉⒶⓋ	T ① ② ③ / A ① ② ③ / V ① ② ③ / i ① ② ③	T ① ② ③ / A ① ② ③ / V ① ② ③ / i ① ② ③	T ① ② ③ ④ / A ① ② ③ ④ / V ① ② ③ ④ / i ① ② ③ ④	T ① ② / A ① ② / V ① ② / i ① ②

NUMBER OF ADULTS IN CLASSROOM   ⓪ ① ② ● ④ ⑤ ⑥ ⑦ ⑧ ⑨ ⑩

Figure 11 continued

The possible activities (e.g., arts and crafts, games, active play) are listed on the left side of the measure. The grouping of the children is indicated by the four columns: One Child, Two Children, Small Groups, Large Groups. The letters (T, A, V, i) under each column stand for *T*eacher, *A*ide, *V*olunteer, and *i*ndependent child. The circled numbers in each column allow the observer to record, as in Figure 11 for instance, that two children are working together on math, unsupervised; two aides are each working with small groups of students in math; and one teacher is supervising a single small group in math. In the box at left center, the observer has indicated that materials in use by the dyad and small groups are texts, workbooks, puzzles and games. Stallings has adapted the classroom observation procedure for use in classrooms from a broad range of educational programs: group process, developmental, exploratory, cognitive, programmed instruction, and fundamental school classroom models.

The third part of the Stallings observation procedure, the 5-minute interaction shown in Figure 12, records interpersonal exchanges among teachers, students, aides, etc., in the classroom. The system categorizes behavioral and verbal interchanges and records their emotional tone (happy, unhappy). The instrument resembles a coded behavior record, and so the observer needs to memorize a fairly complex code. Rather than write down the codes from memory, however, the observer darkens cells on a computer scorable form. The Stallings system comes complete with flashcards to help observers learn the code.

List of Codes

Who/To Whom	What	How
T - Teacher	1 - Command or Request	H - Happy
A - Aide	2 - Open-ended Question	U - Unhappy
V - Volunteer	3 - Response	N - Negative
C - Child	4 - Instruction,	T - Touch
D - Different Child	Explanation	Q - Question
2 - Two Children	5 - Comments, Greetings;	G - Guide/Reason
S - Small Group (3-8)	General Action	P - Punish
L - Large Group (9 up)	6 - Task-related Statement	O - Object
An - Animal	7 - Acknowledge	W - Worth
M - Machine	8 - Praise	DP - Dramatic
	9 - Corrective Feedback	Play/Pretend
	10 - No Response	A - Academic
	11 - Waiting	B - Behavior
	12 - Observing, Listening	
	NV - Nonverbal	
	X - Movement	

R - Repeat the frame
S - Simultaneous action
C - Cancel the frame

Figure 12. List of codes for the "5-minute interaction" in the Stallings observation system

Because of its already considerable use, the care with which it was developed, and its potential applicability, the Stallings observation method is recommended for assessing the implementation of programs where the classroom is the unit of study.

For Further Reading

Boehm, A. E., & Weinberg, R. A. *The classroom observer: A guide for developing observation skills.* New York: Teachers College Press, 1977.

Bowman, G. W., & Mayer, R. S. *BRACE: An instrument for systematic observation of verbal communication and behavior in educational settings.* New York: Bank Street College of Education, 1976.

Evans, W., & Sheffler, J. W. Assessing the implementation of an innovative instructional system. *The Journal of Educational Administration,* 1976, *14*(1), 107-118.

Grady, M. B. Selection criteria for choosing classroom observation instruments. *Contemporary Education,* 1975, *46,* 173-176.

Herbert, J., & Attridge, C. A guide for developers and users of observation systems and manuals. *American Educational Research Journal, 1975, 12(1), 1-20.*

Stallings, J. A. *Learning to look: A handbook on classroom observation and teaching models.* Belmont, CA: Wadsworth Publishing Co., 1977.

Weinberg, R. A., & Wood, F. H. (Eds.). *Observation of pupils and teachers in mainstream and special education settings: Alternative strategies.* Reston, VA: Council for Exceptional Children, 1975.

Chapter 6

Methods For Measuring Program Implementation: Self-Reports

A good way to find out what a program looked like is to *ask* the people involved. You could *interview* the program staff, students, or administrators. You could interview community members to get an idea of the participation of the broader community—particularly if this is one of the program's goals. You could, if you want to reach a large number of people connected with the program, compose and circulate *questionnaires* asking about different peoples' experiences with the program. Interviews and questionnaires are information-collection methods that rely on peoples' *self-reports*, descriptions of their own experiences.

Where there is a plan or theory describing the program, gathering information from staff will involve questioning them about the consistency between program activities as they were planned and as they actually occurred. Where the program has not been prescribed, information from people connected with it will tell you how the program evolved.

Self-reports can be of two types, depending on *when* they are requested. They may consist of:

- *Periodic* reports throughout the course of the program
- *Retrospective* reports at the end of the program

Periodic reports will generally yield more accurate implementation information because they allow respondents to report about program activities soon after they have occurred, when they are still fresh in memory. For this reason, they are nearly always more credible than retrospective reports. Periodic reports should be used even when your role is summative and you are required to describe the program only once, at its conclusion. Retrospective self-reports should be used only when you have no choice, or when the program is small enough or of such short duration that reconstructions after-the-fact will be believable.

The following are step-by-step directions for collecting periodic self-reports through questionnaires or interviews. If you need a retrospective report, adapt these procedures.

How To Gather Periodic Self-Reports Over the Course of the Program

Step 1. Decide how many times you will distribute questionnaires or interviews

As soon as you begin working on the evaluation and as early as possible during the time span of the program, decide how often you will need to collect reports. This decision will be determined by:

- *The homogeneity of program activities.* If each program unit has essentially the same format as the others, then you will not need to "catch" descriptions of particular ones. If every lesson in an American history program, for instance, consists of lecture, reading, and then discussion, then any one lesson you ask about will reflect the program's usual format. In this case, you can plan data collection at your discretion. If the program has some unique parts, say, a field trip to the State Legislature or a seminar on the Constitution, then your data collection will be determined by where these events occur in the program's schedule. Particularly if you are a formative evaluator consulting on program improvements, you will want to ask about these rarer parts of the program as soon as they occur for the first time. This will give you a chance to digest information and give feedback to the planners and staff so that things go more smoothly or people learn more the next time.
- *Your assessment of peoples' tolerance for interruptions.* Unless the program is sparsely staffed, you should not ask for more than three reports from any one individual over the span of a long-term program (e.g., a year). You could *sample,* of course, so that the chances are reduced that any one person will be asked to report often.
- *The amount of time you expect to have available for scoring and interpreting information in reports.*

Once you have decided *when* to collect self-reports, combine this information with your decision about *whom* to ask for reports and complete a sampling plan, as described on pages 60 to 64.

Step 2. Warn people that you will be requesting periodic information

As early during the evaluation as possible, inform staff members and others that in order to measure implementation of their program, you must ask that they provide you with information about how the program looks in operation.

Step 3. Prepare a list of the program's critical features

Procedures for listing the characteristics of the program—materials, activities, administrative arrangements—that you will examine are discussed in Chapter 3, pages 57 to 60.

Step 4. Decide—if you have not already—whether to distribute questionnaires, to interview, or to do both

You probably know about the relative advantages and disadvantages of using questionnaires or interviews. Table 2, page 54, reminds you of some of them. If you are using self-report instruments to supplement program description data from a more credible source—observations or records—then questionnaire data should be sufficient. On the other hand, if self-report measures will provide your only implementation backup data, then you should interview some participants. Unless you are a clever questionnaire writer, you probably cannot find out all you need to know about the program from a pencil-and-paper instrument.

Step 5. Write questions based on the list from Step 3 that will prompt people to tell you what they saw and did as they participated in the program

You want to know how participants *used the materials* and *engaged in the activities* described as comprising the program. To this effect, ask about the following:

a. The *occurrence, frequency,* or *duration* of activities. Whether you collect frequency and duration information in addition to occurrence will depend on the program. To describe a Science Lab program, for instance, you would need merely to determine whether the planned labs occurred at all—and in the correct sequence. If, on the other hand, the program in question consisted of daily, 45-minute English conversation drills, then you would need to know whether the activity occurred with the prescribed frequency and duration.

b. The *form* the activities took. Gathering information on the form of the activities means asking about which students took part in the activities, which materials were used and how often, what activities looked like, and possibly where they occurred. It will also be useful to check whether the form of the activities remained constant or whether the activities changed from time to time or student to student.

c. The *amount of involvement* of participants in these activities. Besides knowing what activities occurred, you should make some check on the extent of interest and participation on the part of the target group—say, the students. Even if activities were set up using the prescribed schedule, students can only be expected to have learned from them if they engaged the students' attention. Were students in a math tutoring program, for instance, mostly working on the prescribed exercises, or were they conversing about sports and clothes some of the time? Were students in an *unstructured* period actually exploring the enrichment materials, or were they just doing their homework? Some of this slippage is inevitable in every program (as in all human endeavor). Still, it is important to find out the extent of non-involvement in the program you are evaluating.

If you intend to design a questionnaire, then you have a choice of two question formats: a closed (*selected*) or open (*constructed*) response format. Ease of scoring and clear reporting lead most evaluators to use *closed-response* questionnaires. On such a questionnaire, the respondent is asked to check or otherwise indicate a *pre-provided answer* to a specific question. Recording the answers involves a simple tally of response categories chosen. On the *open-response* questionnaire, the respondent is asked to write out a short answer to a more general question. The open-response format has the advantage of allowing respondents to freely give information you had not anticipated, but it is time-consuming to score; and unless you have available a large number of readers, it is not practical for any but the smallest evaluations. Most questionnaires ask principally closed-response questions, but add a few open-response options. These allow respondents to volunteer information important to the evaluation but not specifically requested. Figures 13 and 14 show closed-response questionnaires which allow open responses as well. The *Teacher Questionnaire on Materials Use,* Figure 13, requests that teachers list materials used in addition to those mentioned by the questionnaire. The *Peer-Tutoring Program* questionnaire, Figure 14, asks that teachers explain particular responses to multiple-choice items. The questionnaire in Figure 15 uses a closed-response format exclusively.

Interviews too can take several forms, depending on how you ask questions. An interview can be *structured.* Like a closed-response questionnaire, it can be based upon specific questions asked in a prearranged order; neither the questions nor their order are varied across interviewees. An interview can also be *unstructured.* That is, it can ask a few general questions and then encourage the respondent to amplify answers to the questions. The unstructured interview does not need to follow a specific question sequence.

Unstructured interviews, since they resemble conversations and could easily go off track, require not only that you compose a few general questions to stimulate talk, but also that you write *probes*. Probes are short comments to stimulate the respondent to say or remember more, and to guide the interview toward relevant topics:

- *Can you tell me more about that?*
- *Why do you think that happened?*

TEACHER QUESTIONNAIRE ON MATERIALS USE

Teacher's Name_____   Grade_____

Place a check in the appropriate column indicating how often in the course of the program you used the materials and facilities listed in the left-hand column.

Materials	Very often (used almost every day)	Fairly often (used at least once a week)	Seldom (used less than once a week)	Never used
Dial-a-word				
Videotape apparatus				
Animal word game				
Homemade flashcards				
Bozo phonics book				
Magnetic letters				
Phoneme Bingo				
Sunnydate Readers				
Grade 1				
Grade 2				
Sunnydate Workbooks				
Grade 1				
Grade 2				
Please write in additional materials used in your classroom in connection with the XYZ Program:				

Figure 13. A questionnaire about use of program materials. It contains both closed and open response formats.

DOCUMENTATION QUESTIONNAIRE
Peer-Tutoring Program

The following are statements about the peer-tutoring program implemented this year. We are interested in knowing whether they represent
an accurate statement of what the program looked like in operation.
For this reason, we ask that you indicate, using the 1 to 5 scale
after each statement, whether it was "generally true," etc. Please
circle your answer. If you answer seldom or never true, please use
the lines under the statement to correct its inaccuracy.

		always true	gener-ally true	seldom true	never true	don't know
1.	Students were tutored three times a week for periods of 45 minutes each.	1	2	3	4	5
2.	Tutoring took place in the classroom, tutors working with their own classmates.	1	2	3	4	5
3.	Tutors were the fast readers.	1	2	3	4	5
4.	Students were selected for tutoring on the basis of reading grades.	1	2	3	4	5
5.	Tutoring used the "Read and Say" workbooks.	1	2	3	4	5
6.	There were no discipline problems.	1	2	3	4	5

Figure 14. A questionnaire about program activities.
Also uses both closed and open response formats.

DOCUMENTATION QUESTIONNAIRE
Peer-Tutoring Program

Please answer the following questions by placing the letter of the
most accurate response on the line to the left of the question. We
are interested in finding out what the project looked like in operation during the past week, regardless of how it was planned to look.
If more than one answer is true, answer with as many letters as you
need.

_____ 1. On the average, how many times did tutoring sessions take
           place in your classroom?

           a) never   c) 3 or 4 times

           b) 1 or 2 times   d) 5 or more times

_____ 2. What was the average length of a tutoring session?

           a) 5-15 minutes   c) 25-45 minutes

           b) 15-25 minutes   d) longer than 45 minutes

_____ 3. Where in the school did tutoring usually take place?

           a) classroom   c) library

           b) sometimes classroom,   d) room other than classroom
              sometimes other room   or library

_____ 4. Who were the tutors?

           a) only fast students   c) only average students

           b) fast students and some   d) other
              average students

_____ 5. On what basis were tutees selected?

           a) reading achievement   c) general grade average

           b) teacher recommendations d) other

_____ 6. What materials were used by teachers and tutors?

           a) whatever tutors chose   c) "Read and Say" workbooks

           b) specially constructed   d) other
              games

_____ 7. How typical of the program as a whole was last week, as you
           have described it here?

           a) just the same   c) some aspects not typical

           b) almost the same   d) not typical at all

Figure 15. Example of a closed response questionnaire

General questions for the unstructured interview can be phrased in several ways:

- *How often, how many times, or hours a week did the program (or its major features) occur?*
- *What can you tell me about how the activities actually looked–can you recall an instance and describe to me exactly what went on?*
- *How involved did the students seem to be–did all students partici- pate, or were there some students who were always absent or distracted?*
- *I understand that you are attempting to implement a behavior modification, or open classroom, or values clarification program here. What kinds of classroom activities have been suggested to you by this point of view?*

Follow, perhaps, with a probe:

- *What would a stranger walking into your class see going on as a result of your belief that this sort of program should be taking place with students? Be as specific as you can.*

There is no set format for probes. In fact, a good way of probing to gain more complete information from respondents who have forgotten or left something out of their answer might be a simple:

I see. Is there anything else?

You should insert probes whenever the respondent makes a strong state- ment in either an expected or an unexpected direction. For instance, a teacher might say:

Oh, yes. Participation, student involvement was very high–100%.

The best probe for such a strong response is a simple rephrasing and repetition:

Your statement is that every student participated 100% of the time?

This probe leads the respondent to reconsider.

The unstructured interview is like a conversation; the structured inter- view is akin to mutual participation in filling out a questionnaire. Either type is useful for collecting implementation information, depending on what you want to know. An unstructured interview can explore areas of implementation which were unplanned or which evolved differently from the plan. Structured interviews will help you gather corroboration for ideas you already have about how the program looked.

Regardless of whether you construct a questionnaire or interview, write questions in compliance with the pointers in Table 8.

TABLE 8
Some Principles To Follow When Writing Questions For An Instrument To Describe Program Implementation

To ensure usable responses to implementation questions:

1. When possible, ask about specific—and recent—events or time periods such as *today's math lesson, Thursday's field trip, last week*. This persuades people to think concretely about information that should still be fresh in memory. To alleviate your own and the respondent's concern about representativeness of the event, ask for an estimate, and perhaps an explanation, of its typicality.

2. When asking a closed-response question, try to imagine what could have gone wrong with the activities that were planned. Use these possibilities as response alternatives. Resourceful anticipation of likely activity changes will affect the usefulness of the instrument for uncovering changes that did indeed occur. If you feel that you cannot adequately anticipate discrepancies between planned and actual activities, then add "other" as a response alternative and ask respondents to explain.

3. Be sure that you do not *answer* the question by the way you ask it. A good question about what people *did* should not contain a suggestion about how to answer. For instance, questions such as "Were there 4th- and 5th-graders in the program?" or "Did you meet every Monday afternoon?" suggest information you should receive from the respondent. Rather, these questions should be phrased, "What were the grade levels of the students in the program?" "What days of the week and how regularly did you meet?"

4. Identify the frame of reference of the respondents. In an interview, you can learn a great deal from how a person responds as well as from what he says; but when you use a questionnaire, your information will be limited to written responses. The *phrasing* of the questions will therefore be critical. Ask yourself:

   - *What vocabulary would be appropriate to use with this group?*
   - *How well informed are the respondents likely to be?* Sometimes people are perfectly willing to respond to a questionnaire, even when they know little about the subject. They feel they are *supposed* to know, otherwise you would not be asking them. To allow people to express ignorance gracefully, you might include lack of knowledge as a response alternative. Word the alternative so that it does not demean the respondent, for instance, "I have not given much thought to this matter."
   - *Does the group have a particular perspective that must be taken into account—a particular bias?* Try to see the issue through the eyes of the respondents before you begin to ask the questions.

Step 6. Assemble the questionnaire or interview instrument

Arrange questions in a logical order. Do not ask questions that jump from one subject to another.

Compose an introduction. The introduction honors the respondents' right to know why they are being questioned. *Questionnaire* instructions should be specific and unambiguous. Aim for as simple a format as possible. You should assume that a portion of the respondents will ignore instructions altogether. If you feel the format might be confusing, include a conspicuous sample item at the beginning. Instructions for a mailed questionnaire should mention a *deadline* for its return.

Instructions for an interview can be more detailed, of course, and should include reassurances to dilute the respondent's initial apprehension about being questioned. Specifically, the interviewer should:

- *State the purpose of the interview.* Explain what organization you represent, and why you are conducting the evaluation. Explain the purpose of the interview. Describe the report you will have to make regarding the activities that occurred in the program; explain if possible how the information the respondent gives you might affect the program.

- *If the respondent's statements can be kept confidential, say so.* In situations where a social or professional threat to the respondent may be involved, confidentiality of interviews must be stressed and maintained.

- *Explain to the respondent what will be expected during the interview.* For instance, if it will be necessary for the respondent to go back to the classroom to get records, explain the necessity of this action.

Some of the above information should probably be made available to questionnaire respondents as well. This can be done by including a cover letter with the questionnaire.

Step 7. Try out the instrument

Before administering or distributing any instrument, check it out. Give it to one or two people to read aloud, and observe their responses. Have the people explain to you their understanding of what each question is asking. If the questions are not interpreted as you intended, alter them accordingly.

Always rehearse the interviews. Whether you choose to prepare a structured or unstructured interview, once the questions for the interview are selected, the interview should be rehearsed. You, and other interviewers, should run through it once or twice with whoever is available—a wife, a husband, an older child, a secretary. This dry-run is a test of both the instrument and the interviewer. Look for inconsistency in the logic of the question sequencing and difficult or threateningly worded questions. Advise the person who is playing the role of respondent to be as uncooperative as possible to prepare interviewers for unanticipated answers and even hostility.

Step 8. Administer the instrument according to the sampling plan from Step 1

If you *mail questionnaires,* give respondents about two weeks to return them. Then follow up with a reminder, a second mailing, or a phone call if possible. How do you do such a follow-up if people are to respond anonymously? One procedure is to number the return envelopes, check them off a master list as they are returned, remove the questionnaires from the envelopes, and throw the envelopes away.

When distributing any instrument, ask administrators to lend their support. If the instrument carries the sanction of the project director or the school principal, it is more likely to receive the attention of those involved. The superintendent's request for quick returns will carry more authority than yours.

If you *interview,* consider the following suggestions:

- Interviewers should be aware of their influence over what respondents say. Questions about the administration of the program may be answered defensively if staff members fear their answers might make them look bad in a report. Explain to the respondents that the report will refer to no one personally. Understand, as well, that respondents will speak more candidly to interviewers whom they perceive as being like themselves—not representatives of authority.
- Interviewers should have a plan for dealing with reluctant respondents. The best way to overcome resistance is to be explicit about the interview and what it will demand of the respondent.
- If possible, interviews should be recorded—on audiotape to be transcribed at a later time—particularly unstructured ones. Recorded interviews enable you to summarize the information using exact quotes from the respondent; they also require a lot of transcription time. Transcribing the tape in full will take at least half again as long as the interview itself. An alternative is that interviewers *take notes* during an unstructured interview. Notes should include a general summary of each response, with key phrases recorded verbatim. If possible, summaries of unstructured interviews should be returned to respondents so that misunderstandings in the transcription can be corrected.

Step 9. Record data from questionnaires and interview instruments on a data summary sheet

Chapter 3, page 67, described the use of a data summary sheet for recording data from many forms in one place in preparation for data summary and analysis. Data from closed-response items on questionnaires and structured interview schedules can be transferred directly to the data summary sheet. Responses to open-response items and unstructured interviews will have to be summarized before they can be further interpreted. Procedures for reducing a large amount of narrative information by either summarizing or quantifying it were discussed on pages 71 to 73. Even if you plan to write a narrative report of your results, the data summary sheet will show trends in the data that can be described in the narrative.

For Further Reading

Henerson, M. E., Morris, L. L., & Fitz-Gibbon, C. T. How to measure attitudes. In L. L. Morris (Ed.), *Program evaluation kit.* Beverly Hills: Sage Publications, 1978.
This book gives more detailed advice about using questionnaires and interviews as sources of evaluation data.

Kahn, R. L., & Cannell, C. F. *The dynamics of interviewing.* New York: Wiley, 1957.
See in particular, the chapter on "The Formulation of Questions."

Payne, S. L. *The art of asking questions.* Princeton: Princeton University Press, 1951.

Rich, J. *Interviewing children and adolescents.* New York: St. Martins Press, 1968.

Weisberg, H. F., & Bowen, B. D. *An introduction to survey research and data analysis.* San Francisco: W. H. Freeman and Co., 1977.
A general text on conducting surveys.

Chapter 7

The Validity and Reliability of Implementation Measures

The topic of this chapter is the technical adequacy of implementation measures—the validity and reliability of methods used to assess program implementation. The chapter is intended to help you think about the quality of the measures you construct or select to back up your description of a program. Whether you are reading this chapter because you need to assess the quality of a particular instrument or for general information, *think about a concrete situation as you read*—a particular school or classroom familiar to you and perhaps a classroom observation instrument. This will give you something tangible on which to build new information.

If the instrument you have in mind is one which yields *a single summary number* or index (see page 75) to indicate, for instance, the *amount of training* received by classroom aides or the *extent of use* of a certain set of curriculum materials, then your instrument is analogous to an achievement test. When the data are summarized, one score will be reported. Since most cogitation about reliability and validity has been directed toward achievement and ability tests, classical methods for determining technical quality have focused on the many-items-one-score situation.

Instruments for describing implementation, on the other hand, are often scored and interpreted item-by-item: *During the "exploration period," how many students visited the science resource area? What percent of tenth graders refrained from commenting during discussion?* In these cases each question is an individual instrument in itself. It keeps its identity; it is never swallowed up to contribute to any grander score. That single question is the *only* measure made of that program feature in that particular situation. When you consolidate your results from many program sites or times, you compute, say, a single mean to represent your summary of that one item. *In such instances, you need to think about the reliability and validity of each unique item.*

Measurement Validity and Reliability

Assessments of the validity and reliability of a measurement instrument help to determine the amount of faith people should place in its results. *Validity* and *reliability* refer to different aspects of a measure's credibility. Judgments of validity answer the question:

Is the instrument appropriate for what needs to be measured?

Judgments of reliability answer the question:

Does the instrument yield consistent results?

These are questions you must ask about any method you select to back up your description of program implementation. "Valid" has the same root as "valor" and "value"; it indicates how worthwhile a measure is likely to be for telling you what you need to know. Validity boils down to whether the instrument is giving you the true story, or at least something approximating the truth.

When reliability is used to describe a measurement instrument, it carries the same meaning as when it is used to describe friends. A reliable friend is one on whom you can count to behave the *same way time and again.* In this sense, an observation instrument, questionnaire, or interview schedule that gives you essentially the same results when readministered in the same setting is a reliable instrument.

But while reliability refers to *consistency,* consistency does not guarantee *truthfulness.* A friend, for instance, who compliments your taste in clothes *each time she sees you* is certainly reliable but may not necessarily be telling the truth. Further, she may not even be deliberately misleading you. Paying compliments may be a habit, or perhaps her judgment of how you dress may be positively influenced by other good qualities you possess. It may be that by a more objective standard you and your friend have terrible taste in clothes! Similarly, simply because an instrument is reliable does *not* mean that it is a good measure of what it seems to measure.

Will a measure that has been shown to be valid also be reliable? Yes. A valid instrument is one that has demonstrated its ability to detect some "real" situation that its user can identify and characterize. *If the thing being measured—such as a program—is itself stable,* then each administration of a valid instrument should yield essentially the same results. The thing to remember is that a demonstration of reliability is *necessary* but not *conclusive* evidence that an instrument is valid. All the reliability studies in the world will not *guarantee* validity.

Validity: Is the Instrument an Appropriate One For Describing What You Want To Know About the Program?

You are *measuring,* rather than simply *describing* the program on the basis of what someone *says* it looks like, because you want to be able to back up what you say. You are trying to assure both yourself and your audience that the description is an accurate representation of the program as it took place. You want your audience to accept your description as a substitute for having an omniscient view of the program. Such acceptance requires that you anticipate the potential arguments a skeptic might use to dismiss your results. When measuring program implementation, the most frequent argument made by someone skeptical of your description might go something like this:

> Respondents to an implementation questionnaire or subjects of an observation have an idea of what the program is *supposed* to look like *regardless of whether this is what they usually do in fact.* Because they do not wish to appear to deviate, or because they fear reprisals, they will bend their responses or behavior to conform to a model of how they feel they *ought* to appear. Where this happens, the instrument, of course, will not measure the true implementation of the program. Such an instrument will be invalid.

In measuring program implementation, concern over instrument validity boils down to a four-part question: Is the description of the program which the instrument presents *accurate, relevant, representative* and *complete?*[2][3]

An accurate instrument allows the evaluation audience to create for themselves a picture of a program that is close to what they would have gained had they actually seen the program. A relevant implementation measure calls attention to the *most critical features* of the program—those which are most likely related to the program's outcomes and which someone wishing to replicate the program would be most interested in knowing about.

A *representative* description of program implementation will present a *typical* depiction of the program and its sundry variations as they appeared across sites and over time. A *complete* picture of the program is one that includes *all* the relevant and important program features.

Making a case for accuracy and relevance

You can defend the *accuracy* of your depiction of the program by ruling out charges that there is purposeful bias or distortion in the information.

---

23. The question of accuracy and relevance reflects a concern for traditional *construct* validity; representativeness and completeness refer to *content* validity. The four concerns, of course, overlap. Satisfying one will contribute greatly to addressing the others.

There are various ways to guard against such charges. Self-report instruments, for example, can be anonymous. If you are using observations, you can demonstrate that the observers have nothing to gain by a particular outcome and that the events they have witnessed were not contrived for their benefit. Records kept over the course of the program are particularly easy to defend on this account if they are complete and have been checked periodically against the program events they record. You need only show that the people extracting the information from the records are unbiased.

You can, in addition, show that administration procedures are *standardized,* that is, that the instrument has been used in the same way every time. Make sure that:

- Enough time was allowed to respondents, observers, or recorders so that the use of the instrument was not rushed

- Pressure to respond in a particular way was absent from the instrument's format and instructions, from the setting of its administration, and from the personal manner of the administrator

Another way to argue that your description is accurate is to show that results from any one of your instruments coincide logically with results from other implementation measures.

You can also add support to a case that your instrument is accurate by presenting evidence that it is *reliable.* Though it is usually difficult to demonstrate statistically that an implementation instrument is reliable, a good case for reliability can be based on the instrument's having *several items that examine each of the program's most critical features.* Measuring something important, say the amount of time students spend per day reading silently, by means of one item only, exposes your report to potential error from response formulation and interpretation. You can correct this by including several items whose results can be combined to compile an *index* (see page 75), or by administering the item several times to the same person.

If *experts* feel that a profile produced by an implementation instrument hits major features of the program or program component you intend to describe, then this is strong evidence that your data are *relevant.* For instance, a classroom description would need to include the curriculum used, the amount of time spent on instruction per unit per day, etc. A district-wide program, on the other hand, might need to focus heavily on key administrative arrangements for the program.

Making a case for representativeness and completeness

To demonstrate representativeness and completeness, you must show that in *administering* the instrument you did not omit any sites or time periods in which program implementation may have looked different. You must also show that you have not given too much emphasis to a single atypical variation of the program. Thus your data must sample program sites typical of each of the different places where the program has been implemented. Your sample should also account for different times of the day, or different times during the life of the program if these are variations likely to be of concern. The variations you have been able to detect must represent the range of those that occurred.

As you can see, there is no one established method for determining validity. Any combination of the types of evidence described here can be used to support validity. If you plan to use an implementation instrument more than once, consider the whole period of its use an opportunity to collect information about the accuracy of the picture it gives you. Each administration is a chance to collect the opinions of experts, to assess the consistency of the view that this instrument gives you with that from other instruments, etc. Establishing instrument validity should be a continuing process.

Reliability: Does the Instrument Produce Consistent Results?

Reliability refers to the extent to which measurement results are free of unpredictable kinds of error. For example, if you were to give students a math test one day and, without additional instruction, give them the same test two days later, you would expect each student to receive more or less the same score. If this should turn out *not* to be the case, you would have to conclude that your instrument is *unreliable,* because, without instruction, a person's knowledge of math does not fluctuate much from day to day. If the score fluctuates, the problem must be with the test. Its results must be influenced by things other than math knowledge. These other things are called *error.*

Sources of error that affect the reliability of tests, questionnaires, interviews, etc., include:

- Fluctuations in the mood or alertness of respondents because of illness, fatigue, recent good or bad experiences, or other temporary differences among members of the group being measured.

- Variations in the conditions of use from one administration to the next. These range from various distractions, such as unusual outside noises, to inconsistencies and oversights in giving directions.

- Differences in scoring or interpreting results, chance differences in what an observer notices, and errors in computing scores.

- Random effects caused by examinees or respondents who guess or check off alternatives without trying to understand them.

Methods for demonstrating an instrument's reliability—whether the instrument is long and intricate or composed of a single question—usually involve comparing the results of one administration of the instrument with another by correlating[24] them. Sometimes this reliability is estimated by first administering the instrument to a group of people and then readministering the test to the same people at some later point in time. This method is called *test-retest* reliability. Sometimes an *alternate form* of the test is administered to the same people to yield an estimate of alternate-form reliability. Sometimes, when the items on an instrument are all similar or can be divided into similar groups, results from the instrument's items are divided into half; and each equivalent half of the instrument is compared to the other to estimate how internally consistent the instrument is—whether its items all give similar results. This is the method of *split-half* reliability.[25]

The evaluator designing and using instruments for measuring program implementation has unique problems when attempting to demonstrate reliability. Most of these problems stem from the fact that implementation instruments aim at characterizing a situation rather than measuring some quality of a person. While a person's skill, say in basic math, can be expected to stay constant long enough for assessment of test reliability to take place, a program cannot be expected to hold still so that it can be measured. Because the program will likely be dynamic rather than static, possibilities for test-retest and alternate form reliability are usually ruled out. And since most instruments used for measuring implementation are actually collections of single items which independently measure different things, the possibility of computing split-half reliabilities practically never occurs. In sum:

While classical test construction assumes that the underlying characteristic being measured remains stable and only the precision of measuring it varies, no such assumption can be made for any measurement of classroom characteristics.[26]

---

24. Correlation refers to the strength of the relationship between two measures. A high *positive* correlation means that people scoring high on one measure also score high on the other. A low correlation means that knowing a person's score on one measure does not educate your guess about his score on the other. Correlations are usually expressed by a *correlation coefficient,* a decimal between −1 and +1, calculated from people's scores on the two measures. Since there are several different correlation coefficients, each depending on the types of instruments being used, discussion of how to perform correlations to determine validity or reliability is outside the scope of this book. The various correlation coefficients are discussed in most statistics texts, however. You might also refer to *How To Calculate Statistics,* part of the *Program Evaluation Kit.*

25. Methods for determining instrument reliability are discussed in most research texts, such as those listed in the For Further Reading Section at the end of the chapter.

26. Leinhardt, G. Evaluating an adaptive education program: Implementation to replication. *Instructional Science, Vol. 6.* Amsterdam: Elsevier Scientific Publishing Co., 1977 (p. 232).

Because of the problem of situational instability, it might be difficult for you to determine the reliability of implementation measures.[27] And where you *can* calculate reliability, it may look artificially low. This does not, of course, mean that your instruments cannot be reliable; it means that it will be difficult to use standard statistical methods to demonstrate that they *are*. However, since the ultimate and most important quality of a measurement instrument is that it be valid, demonstrating that your instruments are valid will eliminate the need to show that they are reliable.

Inter-rater Reliability

Observation instruments and unstructured interviews—in fact, any measures that rely upon someone's judgment—have chronic credibility problems which are related to the issue of reliability. With these data collection methods the *instrument,* to a large extent, is a *person;* and the perceptions of this person may fluctuate. For example, during a Monday observation, an observer might see a teacher pick up a student's worksheet and say: "Robert! Have you done so much already?" The observer might interpret this particular teacher behavior as *asking a question.* On Tuesday the same rater might observe the same behavior and interpret it as *making a statement of praise.*

With observations, the best way to demonstrate that your evaluation has been minimally contaminated by inconsistency from "human instruments" is to use more than one observer. If different people report behavior or activities in essentially the same way, then you have evidence that the rules for recording have been well learned and uniformly applied.

If you are using interviews, you should conduct tryouts to verify that different interviewers questioning the same person will come up with the same answers.

If your instrument is an observation measure or interview, and you will be using only a *single* reporter, you can estimate this observer's reliability in the following way:

- First, videotape or film part of an episode which the observer will be coding.
- Then, train *another person,* who will act as a reliability check, to observe in the *same way* as your observer. Have this person watch and code the film or videotape. The reliability which you are able to

---

27. On the other hand, since correlating results from two administrations of an instrument is not a taxing procedure, you might want to try calculating some reliability coefficients. For help with this, see Henerson, M., Morris, L. L., & Fitz-Gibbon, C. T. How to measure attitudes. Fitz-Gibbon, C. T., & Morris, L. L. How to calculate statistics. In L. L. Morris (Ed.), *Program evaluation kit.* Beverly Hills: Sage Publications, 1978. See also Talmage, H. *Statistics as a tool for educational practitioners.* Berkeley, CA: McCutchan Publishing Co., 1976.

calculate by correlating these two observations will give you an idea of the consistency with which your one observer can be counted on to record accurately the information obtained.

Incidentally, if you will be able to have *more than one rater observe each event* during actual data collection, it is good practice to include in your evaluation report the *mean* results calculated across raters. Because this information comes from more than one source, it will be more reliable than separate reports.

Calculating inter-rater reliability

When observations are used, you will need to demonstrate reliability by having your observers watch the *same* behavioral episode and then submit their recorded results for comparison.

If you have *two* observers only, and they will be attending to a few specific events rather than characterizing what goes on in, say, a whole room, then you can probably show inter-rater reliability by means of a *correlation.* A high correlation (roughly .70 or above) shows that the measurement method is sufficiently reliable. Lower correlations indicate that the observers or reporters do not agree about what they are reporting, and you should be correspondingly skeptical about the accuracy of the data.

Table 9 shows a way to display data to begin calculating a correlation coefficient of inter-rater reliability. Table 9 directs you to compare two observers' answers to each of the items on the instrument. Down the lefthand column, you should list the items on the instrument. X should be Observer X's responses to the item; Y should be Observer Y's. If your observation instrument consists of a delayed report questionnaire or a checklist, then the item entered in the columns under X and Y will be quantities tallied from the observers' responses or the checklists. If you anticipate difficulty reducing the items to single numbers, or if the instrument yields different sorts of numbers—perhaps some *tallies* of quantities of materials and some ratings of student behaviors—then you will need to convert all of the numbers to the same scale.

The sorts of data that implementation measures can produce are of three types:

1. *Nominal* data are classifications of cases into categories with names but no particular order; for example, yes/no, present/absent, had inservice/ did not, like/dislike, ABC reading series/Urban readers/See-and-Say reading series.

2. *Ordinal* measures provide values which arrange people in some kind of order. But although they place things in order, ordinal data do not tell you how far apart they are. For example, if a person falls into a middle

TABLE 9
Data Displayed so that
a Correlation Coefficient Can Be Calculated

Observation instrument item or rating categories	Observer or Rater X	Observer or Rater Y
1		
2		
3		
4		
5		

category, it does not mean that she is equally distant from the adjacent categories above and below. If the frequency of use of materials in a program is reported in terms of never/rarely/sometimes/frequently/always, for instance, you cannot assume that the difference between rarely and sometimes is the same size as the difference between frequently and always. Other examples of ordinal scales are low/moderate/high degree of implementation, and *rank* along some dimension.

3. *Interval* measures, on the other hand, provide values along a scale consisting of equal intervals; these measures show you the amount of something. The difference between any two adjacent values is assumed to be equal to the difference between any other two adjacent values. Tallies and counts, and estimes of amount or percent of time, interest, or effort produce interval data.

You can calculate a correlation by reducing results from more complex data types *down* to simpler form. If you have an instrument made up of interval and ordinal items, you can convert the interval data to ordinal which will provide you with two sets of ordinal data for which you can calculate a correlation coefficient.[28] If you have an instrument with

---

28. Recently, some authors have nominated a correlation-like statistic, Cohen's Kappa, as a substitute for more standard correlation coefficients when calculating inter-rater reliabilities with nominal or interval data. The statistic is easy to calculate and interpret, but only if data have been entered into the equation properly. It is suggested that you explore methods for showing inter-rater reliability by conferring with a data analyst. Specific references to Cohen's Kappa can be found in Cohen, J. A coefficient of agreement for nominal scales. *Educational and Psychological Measurement*, 1960, *20*, 37-46. See also Fleiss, J. L. *Statistical methods for rates and proportions*. New York: John Wiley & Sons, 1973.

nominal and interval items, you can convert the interval data to nominal, again giving you two sets of data on the same kind of scale. Since the conversion procedure can be intricate, you may have to consult a data analyst or a text on measurement to perform this task.

If you will use *more than two* observers or raters, *or* if your two raters will observe several events, *or* if they will record many different features of what they see, then it will be appropriate to estimate interrater reliability using analysis of variance (ANOVA) rather than a correlation.[2 9] Since the form of ANOVA you use will depend on your situation, and since the best way to perform the ANOVA is by computer, you should consult a data analyst to help you in this case.

For Further Reading

Anastasi, A. *Psychological testing.* New York: Macmillan, 1968.

Cronbach, L. J. *Essentials of psychological testing.* New York: Harper & Row, 1970.

Cronbach, L. J. Test validation. In R. L. Thorndike (Ed.), *Educational measurement.* Washington, D.C.: American Council on Education, 1970.

Fitz-Gibbon, C. T., & Morris, L. L. How to calculate statistics. In L. L. Morris (Ed.), *Program evaluation kit.* Beverly Hills: Sage Publications, 1978.

Talmage, H. *Statistics as a tool for educational practitioners.* Berkeley: McCutchan Publishing Co., 1976.

---

29. Analysis of variance is discussed briefly in Fitz-Gibbon, C. T., & Morris, L. L. How to design a program evaluation. In L. L. Morris (Ed.), *Program evaluation kit.* Beverly Hills: Sage Publications, 1978. A discussion of the use of ANOVA for the specific purpose of estimating inter-rater reliability can be found in Ebel, R. L. Estimation of the reliability of ratings. *Psychometrika,* 1951, *16,* 407-424. See also Medley, D. M. & Mitzel, H. E. Application of analysis of variance to the estimation of the reliability of observations of teachers' classroom behavior. *Journal of Experimental Education,* 1958, *27,* 23-25.

Index